TRY OUR APP

It's easy to keep up on every issue of BLOCK magazine. Access it from all your devices. And when you subscribe to BLOCK, it's free with your subscription! For the app search BLOCK magazine in the app store. Available for both Apple and Android.

EXECUTIVE EDITORS
Mike Mifsud, Alan Doan, Jenny Doan, Sarah Galbraith, David Mifsud

MANAGING EDITOR
Natalie Earnheart

CREATIVE DIRECTOR
Christine Ricks

PHOTOGRAPHY TEAM
Mike Brunner, Lauren Dorton, Jennifer Dowling, Dustin Weant

PATTERN TEAM
Edie McGinnis, Denise Lane, Tyler Macbeth

PROJECT DESIGN TEAM
Jenny Doan, Natalie Earnheart, Janet Yamamoto

EDITOR & COPYWRITERS
Jenny Doan, Natalie Earnheart, Christine Ricks, Katie Mifsud, Camille Maddox, Nichole Spravzoff, Edie McGinnis, David Litherland

SEWIST TEAM
Jenny Doan, Natalie Earnheart, Janet Yamamoto, Carol Henderson, Denise Lane, Janice Richardson, Jamey Stone

QUILTING & BINDING DEPARTMENT
Sarah Richardson, Betty Bates, Karla Zinkand, Natalie Loucks, Debbie Elder, Jan Meek, Angela Wilson, Chelsea White, Mary McPhee, Charlene McCabe, Dennis Voss, Debbie Allen, Jamee Gilgour, Michelle Templeton, Frank Jones, Kara Snow, Ethan Lucas, Devin Ragle, Bruce VanIperen, Lyndia Lovell, Aaron Crawford, Cyera Cottrill, Deborah Warner, Salena Smiley, Francesca Flemming, Rachael Joyce, Bernice Kelly, Deloris Burnett

LOCATION CREDIT
Kat (Tula's mom) and Larry Runyan Home, Stewartsville, MO
Galbraith Home, Hamilton MO

PRINTING COORDINATORS
Rob Stoebener, Seann Dwyer

PRINTING SERVICES
Walsworth Print Group
803 South Missouri
Marceline, MO 64658

CONTACT US
Missouri Star Quilt Company
114 N Davis
Hamilton, MO 64644
888-571-1122
info@missouriquiltco.com

6 GRAND SQUARE/ DO SI DO

16 TOWN SQUARE

24 BARGELLO

32 TWINKLING STARS

EASY HALF - HEXAGON 40

JOSH'S STAR 48

RHOMBUS STAR 56

FENCE RAIL STARS 64

content

72 FALL SHENANIGANS

80 GRANDMOTHER'S FAN

90 CUT THE APRON STRINGS

92 PENNANT BANNER

IPOD HOLDER 94

BLIPPER 96

EASY HOLIDAY WREATHS 98

Oops! Sometimes we make mistakes. To find corrections to every issue of Block go to: **www.msqc.co/corrections**

hello

Every summer here in Missouri, we hold a Christmas in July retreat. To surprise the retreat-goers, Ron and I like to don our Santa and Mrs. Claus suits and spread cheer throughout the room! Despite the sweltering weather, it always makes me smile to put on that red dress and white apron with matching hat and striped stockings. Even though the holidays are still months away, it gets my creative juices flowing and reminds me of the fun gifts I'd like to stitch up for family and friends. It's always a good idea to get going before the Christmas hustle and bustle. And don't mind me if I happen to sing along to my favorite holiday tunes while I'm at it!

From Halloween to New Year's Eve, each holiday has something to love. I always look forward to answering the door for sweet, little trick-or-treaters in their darling costumes. Thanksgiving is one of my favorite times of the entire year with family gathered around as we express gratitude and eat plenty of turkey. And to cap it all off, Christmas, with its anticipation and joy, fills my heart to the brim for the rest of the year.

This issue of BLOCK has projects for all of these wonderful holidays and more! However you celebrate the holiday season, we want to give you all the inspiration and motivation you need to make it truly memorable for you and your loved ones.

JENNY DOAN
MISSOURI STAR QUILT CO

For the tutorial and everything you need to make this quilt visit: www.msqc.co/holidayblock18

grand square

When you're an adult, December is a blur! There are presents to buy and wrap, parties to attend, cookies to bake, Christmas cards to send, and, of course, quilts to finish—all before December 25th!

But for a child, the weeks before Christmas pass so slowly it can feel like the hourglass is filled with molasses instead of sand. Sometimes it seems like Santa will never arrive!

Our Event Manager, Meg, told us a story about a friend with a very resourceful mother. When Meg's friend was a little girl, the anticipation for Christmas morning was almost more than she could bear. She and her siblings could not wait to discover their Christmas surprises, even if it meant doing a bit of forbidden detective work. Lucky for them, their parents always shopped early and placed the wrapped presents under the tree.

At the first opportunity, those kids would sneak into the living room, as quiet as mice, to either hunt down or seek out the gifts with their names attached. They poked and prodded each package. They shook and checked the weight of every box. They carefully—ever so carefully—pulled back bits of tape to get a glimpse under the wrapping.

Inevitably, their mother would discover their antics and scold them for their mischief. She hated to have the magic of Christmas ruined by their snooping. So, one year she got smart. Instead of labeling the gifts with the children's names, the gift tags were addressed to Dasher, Dancer, Prancer, and so on.

On Christmas morning, the children discovered that each of their stockings had been labeled with the name of a reindeer. It was then, and only then, that they knew which gifts were theirs. So, for the first time in many years, they opened their presents and were genuinely surprised by the fun they found inside.

When asked about her childhood memories, our Pattern Writer, Edie McGinnis shared this cute story about one of her favorite Christmases:

"My sisters and I got up one Christmas morning, went racing into the living room and found nothing under the tree except three balls of string, partly unwound, trailing around the room. Each ball of string had a slip of paper with a name on it. That was it. We didn't know whether to laugh or cry.

My dad had a big grin on his face and said, "Go ahead, girls. Pick up your ball of string and see where it leads!"

We each got busy, winding up our string and following the trail.

My oldest sister, Shari, was the fastest. We heard her whooping and hollering out in the yard. It wasn't long before Alice and I joined her and found the end of our ball of string tied to a shiny new bike. Best. Christmas. Ever."

The years pass and many memories fade, but the magic of a childhood Christmas is something we never forget.

materials

QUILT SIZE
61" x 61"

BLOCK SIZE
12" finished

SUPPLIES
2 packages 5" print squares -
  must include duplicate prints
2 yards background fabric -
  includes inner border

OUTER BORDER
1 yard

BINDING
¾ yard

BACKING
4 yards - vertical seam(s)

SAMPLE QUILT
Winter Wonderland by Cheryl Haynes
for Benartex Fabrics

1 cut

Select 4 matching squares for each block. Trim 1 square to 4½". Trim 2 squares into 2½" x 4½" rectangles for a **total of 4**, and 1 square into (4) 2½" squares. Stack all matching pieces together. Repeat for the remaining 15 blocks.

From the background fabric, cut:

- (8) 4½" strips across the width of the fabric – subcut each strip into 4½" squares. Each strip will yield 8 squares and a **total of 64** are needed.

- (4) 2½" strips across the width of the fabric – subcut each strip into 2½" squares. Each strip will yield 16 squares and a **total of 64** are needed.

2 block construction

Sew a 2½" print square to a 2½" background square. Add a matching 2½" strip to one side. This makes up the corner unit of each block. **Make 4.** 2A

Sew a corner unit to either side of a 4½" background square. **Make 2 rows** as shown. 2B

Sew a 4½" background square to either side of a print square that matches the corner unit print.
Make 1 row as shown. 2C

Sew the 3 rows together to complete the block. **Make 16.** 2D

Block Size: 12" finished

3 arrange and sew

Lay out the blocks in rows of 4. **Make 4 rows.** Press the seam allowances of the odd rows toward the left and the even rows toward the right to make the seams "nest." Sew the rows together to complete the center of the quilt.

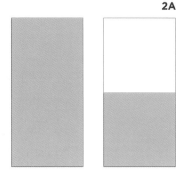

2A

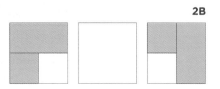

2B

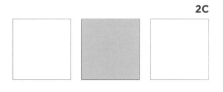

2C

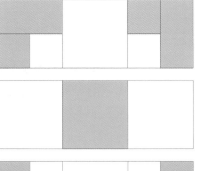

2D

4 inner border

Cut (5) 2½" strips across the width of the fabric. Sew the strips together end-to-end to make one long strip. Trim the borders from this strip

Refer to Borders (pg. 110) in the Construction Basics to measure and cut the inner borders. The strips are approximately 48½" for the sides and approximately 52½" for the top and bottom.

5 outer border

Cut (6) 5" strips across the width of the fabric. Sew the strips together end-to-end to make one long strip. Trim the borders from this strip.

Refer to Borders (pg. 110) in the Construction Basics to measure and cut the outer borders. The strips are approximately 52½" for the sides and approximately 61½" for the top and bottom.

6 quilt and bind

Layer the quilt with batting and backing and quilt. After the quilting is complete, square up the quilt and trim away all excess batting and backing. Add binding to complete the quilt. See Construction Basics (pg. 110) for binding instructions.

Bonus Project:

do si do

You will have some 5" squares left over after making the Grand Square quilt. Here's a cute quilt that uses them up!

QUILT SIZE
45½" x 45½"

BLOCK SIZE
11½" finished

SUPPLIES
(36) 5" squares*
1¼ yards background fabric –
    includes inner border

OUTER BORDER
1¼ yards

BINDING
½ yard

BACKING
3 yards - vertical seam(s)

*Note: you will have 20 squares left over from the packages of squares used when making the Grand Square quilt. Cut the remaining squares needed from the outer border fabric. if you prefer, you can just use a new package of 5" squares to make this quilt.

1 cut

From the outer border fabric, cut:

- (2) 5" strips across the width of the fabric – subcut each strip into 5" squares. Each strip will yield 8 squares and you need a **total of 16.** Stack these squares with the 20 squares you have left over from the Grand Square quilt.

Select 4 print squares for each block. Trim 1 square to 4½". Trim 2 squares into 2½" x 4½" rectangles for a **total of 4**, and 1 square into (4) 2½" squares. Repeat for the remaining 8 blocks.

From the background fabric, cut:

- (5) 4½" strips across the width of the fabric – subcut each strip into 4½" squares. Each strip will yield 8 squares and a **total of 36** are needed.

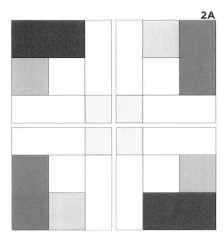

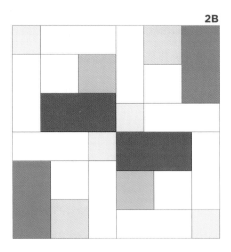

(3) 2½" strips across the width of the fabric – subcut each strip into 2½" squares. Each strip will yield 16 squares and a **total of 36** are needed.

2 block construction

Refer to the block construction directions on page 10 and **make 10 blocks**. Use what you have on hand and don't be concerned about matching up the squares and strips for the corners.

Slice each block in half vertically and horizontally. 2A

Turn 2 corners in toward the center. Sew the block back together. **Make 9.** 2B

Block Size: 11½" finished

3 arrange and sew

Lay out the blocks in rows of 3. **Make 3 rows.** Press the seam allowances of the odd rows toward the left and the even rows toward the right to make the seams "nest." Sew the rows together to complete the center of the quilt.

4 inner border

Cut (4) 1½" strips across the width of the fabric. Sew the strips together end-to-end to make one long strip. Trim the borders from this strip.

Refer to Borders (pg. 110) in the Construction Basics to measure and cut the inner borders. The strips are approximately 35" for the sides and approximately 37" for the top and bottom.

5 outer border

Cut (5) 5" strips across the width of the fabric. Sew the strips together end-to-end to make one long strip. Trim the borders from this strip.

Refer to Borders (pg. 110) in the Construction Basics to measure and cut the outer borders. The strips are approximately 37" for the sides and approximately 46" for the top and bottom.

6 quilt and bind

Layer the quilt with batting and backing and quilt. After the quilting is complete, square up the quilt and trim away all excess batting and backing. Add binding to complete the quilt. See Construction Basics (pg. 110) for binding instructions.

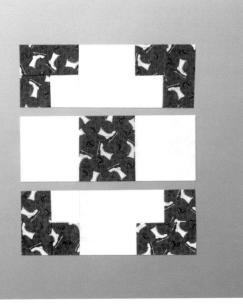

1   Sew a 2½" print square to a 2½" background square. Add a matching 2½" strip to one side to make up the corner unit.

2   Sew a corner unit to either side of a 4½" background square to make the first and third row of the block.

3   Stitch a 4½" background square to either side of a matching print square to make the center row.

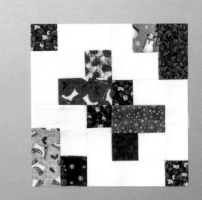

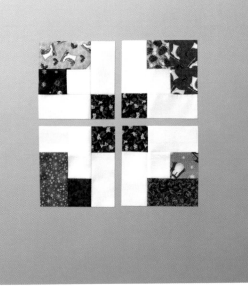

4   Sew the 3 rows together to complete 1 block.

5   Use leftover squares, mix in squares cut from background and border fabrics and don't worry about matching pieces when making our bonus quilt. Follow the directions on page 10 to make the block. Cut it through the middle horizontally and vertically.

6   Turn the upper left quadrant and the lower right quadrant in toward the center. Sew the block back together to create a brand new look!

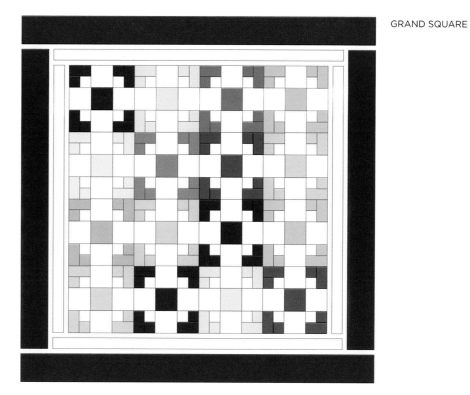

GRAND SQUARE

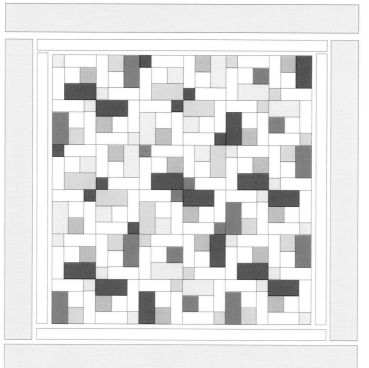

DO SI DO

town square

When my son, Alan, was only nineteen years old, he spent a Christmas away in Ukraine, and boy, did I miss him. I didn't know many details of his long, wintry days in that far-off place, and I wondered what it was like there. Were the people friendly? Did they wish each other a Merry Christmas? Did lights twinkle in the windows? Would my carefully wrapped present arrive in time? And most importantly, would he know how much we loved and missed him?

In our letters, he explained to me that the harsh winters in Ukraine are akin to a winter storm in the Eastern United States. The snow piles up, practically to the knees, and remains intact until spring. Gray days string together and the streets are filled with quietly bustling people in thick, multicolored fur coats, with fur caps atop their heads. And just when the days seem the darkest, suddenly, bright lights appear overhead, strung across wide streets, adorning trees and formal, austere buildings. The city square becomes a wonderland, with a heavily adorned Christmas tree right in the center.

As December 25th approaches, the country just seems to be catching the holiday spirit, as they tend to celebrate the Gregorian calendar dates of the holiday, which fall in January. Bushy, wild-looking Christmas trees line the side streets and markets during the last week of December and are carried off to cozy apartments all over the city where they fill the tiny, fogged windows. It's not uncommon to see a tree being hoisted overhead by a burly man and carried away on his back, instead of being carefully strapped to the top of a midsize car, which most people there don't have.

And the food! Vibrant, red borscht with a thick spoonful of sour cream and a sprinkling of greens looks so festive, and tastes so delicious. Then there's crispy potato pancakes, plump meat dumplings called pelmeni, buttery thin pancakes with sweet and savory fillings, and a steaming metal samovar filled with hibiscus tea, all surrounding a beautifully braided egg bread in the center of the table, sprinkled generously with poppy seeds.

When Santa Claus arrives, don't expect a jolly man in a red suit. The Eastern European "Santa" is a tall, thin man in a light blue suit, without a bag at all, called "Grandfather Frost." He holds a white staff and is often accompanied by his niece, the Snow Maiden. They distribute small gifts and well-wishes, but not before the children give some token of appreciation, like a song or a poem, which they have memorized. Then, everyone gathers around the table, eating and drinking until the wee hours of the morning, punctuating the conversation with calls of "Shchaslyvoho Rizdva!" or "Merry Christmas!"

When I finally got on the phone with my son, after waiting patiently for his old party-line telephone to connect, I was relieved, overjoyed, and just happy to hear his voice say, "Hey, Mom!" Knowing he was safe and well meant the world to us, even though he was still a continent away. The spirit of Christmas brought us together and we passed the phone around to the entire family, celebrating the simple joys of the season.

For the tutorial and everything you need to make this quilt visit:
www.msqc.co/holidayblock18

materials

QUILT SIZE
68" X 86"

BLOCK SIZE
18" finished

QUILT TOP
1 roll 2½" print strips
1¾ yards black fabric – includes inner border

OUTER BORDER
1¼ yard

BINDING
¾ yard

BACKING
5¼ yards - vertical seam(s)

SAMPLE QUILT
Seeing Stars Grunge Metallics by BasicGrey for Moda Fabrics

1 cut

From the black fabric, cut:

- (6) 6½" strips across the width of the fabric – subcut each strip into (6) 6½" squares for a **total of 36**.

2 make strip sets

Sew 3 strips together along the length of the strips with right sides facing to make a strip set. Position the lightest strip on either the top or bottom of the set. **Make 12 sets.**

From each strip set, cut:

- (2) 6½" x 12½" rectangles and (2) 6½" squares. A **total of 24** of each size are needed for the quilt. Stack all matching pieces together. **2A**

3 block construction

Use a stack of matching pieces, and sew a 6½" black square to a 6½" x 12½" strip set. **Make 2 rows** as shown. **3A**

Sew a 6½" strip-pieced square to both sides of a black 6½" square. **Make 1 row** as shown. **3B**

Sew the 3 rows together as shown to complete the block. Notice that the lightest strip always touches the center black square. **Make 12. 3C**

Block Size: 18" finished

4 arrange and sew

Lay out the blocks in rows. Each row is made up of **3 blocks** and **4 rows** are needed. After the blocks have been sewn into rows, press the seam allowances of the odd-numbered rows toward the right and the even-numbered rows toward the left to make the seams "nest."

Sew the rows together to complete the center of the quilt.

3A

3B

3C

5 inner border

Cut (7) 2½" strips across the width of the fabric. Sew the strips together end-to-end to make one long strip. Trim the borders from this strip.

Refer to Borders (pg. 110) in the Construction Basics to measure and cut the outer borders. The strips are approximately 72½" for the sides and approximately 58½" for the top and bottom.

6 outer border

Cut (8) 5½" strips across the width of the fabric. Sew the strips together end-to-end to make one long strip. Trim the borders from this strip.

Refer to Borders (pg. 110) in the Construction Basics to measure and cut the outer borders. The strips are approximately 76½" for the sides and approximately 68½" for the top and bottom.

7 quilt and bind

Layer the quilt with batting and backing and quilt. After the quilting is complete, square up the quilt and trim away all excess batting and backing. Add binding to complete the quilt. See Construction Basics (pg. 110) for binding instructions.

1 Sew (3) 2½" strips together along the length to make a strip set. Always place the lightest strip at the top or bottom of the set.

2 Make the 2 outer rows of the block by sewing a 6½" black square to a 6½" x 12½" strip set.

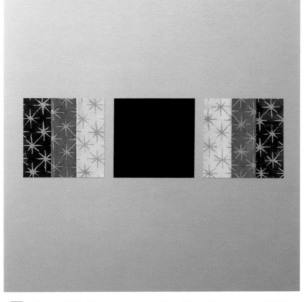

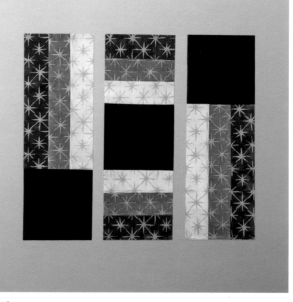

3 Sew a 6½" strip-piece square to either side of a black 6½" square. Make sure the lightest part of the strip set pieces are touching the black square.

4 Sew the outer rows to the center as shown to complete the block. Notice the lighter strips touch the black portion of the center row.

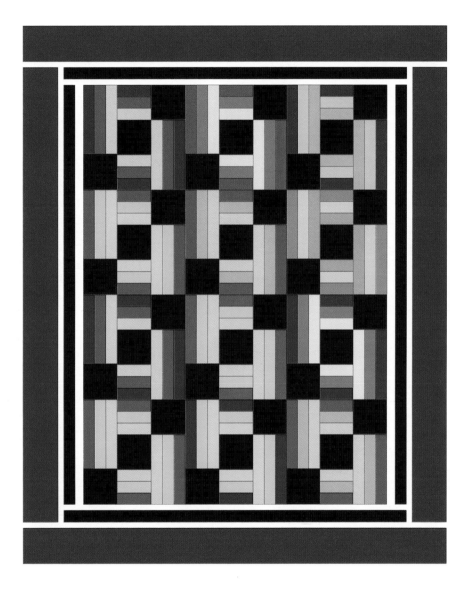

bargello

It's beginning to look a lot like Christmas—and autumn is just around the corner! Christmas decorations used to pop up in stores right around Thanksgiving, but lately, it seems we go to sleep on Halloween night and wake up to all things Christmas!

Some folks embrace the early arrival of the holiday season, while others won't put up the tree until mid December. When does the Christmas season really begin for you? And how do you know it has arrived?

For twin brothers Shane and Rick, Christmas starts with one important treat: eggnog! Growing up, that thick, creamy beverage with just a hit of nutmeg was a Christmas-only treat so beloved, they dreamed about it all year long.

Every year, as the holidays approached, the boys watched like hawks for that first container of eggnog to show up at the store. When they got older, things got competitive. Whoever found the first eggnog of the season was treated to a steak dinner by the other.

The year that Rick moved across the country for law school and Shane was teaching at the local community college, both twins were so wrapped up in work and studies, their annual eggnog competition was all but forgotten.

At the time, Shane was dating a wonderful gal named Leslie. She was smart and beautiful, and a whole lot of fun, but he wanted Rick to meet her in person before he made any big decisions.

One night, Leslie ran to the store to grab a roll of cookie dough for a movie night with Shane when she noticed a display of eggnog on the bottom shelf. She paused for a minute, grabbed a quart, pried open the lid, and dialed Rick's number.

A thousand miles away, Rick was surprised to see Leslie's name pop up on his phone. They'd never talked, just texted a bit. "What's up?" he answered, but the only sound he heard was, gulp, gulp, gulp *gasp* gulp, gulp, gulp, then a hearty, "Eggnog's here!" Without as much as a giggle or goodbye, Leslie hung up the phone and went to pay for her cookie dough and half-empty quart of eggnog.

Meanwhile, Shane, oblivious to what had just happened, got a call from Rick. "Hey Bro, listen. You are going to marry that girl. I'm paying for the steak dinner anyway, so you'd better get a ring and a proposal speech ready, 'cuz she's the one!"

For the tutorial and everything you need to make this quilt visit:
www.msqc.co/holidayblock18

materials

QUILT SIZE
50" X 61½"

QUILT TOP
1 roll of 2½" shaded solid strips
   – the roll you choose must have
   at least 3 strips each of 12 different
   color values.
Note: while you may have 3 pieces of red that
all appear to be the same color value, the print
may vary. That will work just fine!

¾ yards contrasting fabric

BORDER
¾ yard

BINDING
¾ yard or use left over 2½" strips to
make multi-colored binding

BACKING
3¼ yards – horizontal seam(s)

SAMPLE QUILT
Vintage Holiday by Bonnie and
Camille for Moda Fabrics

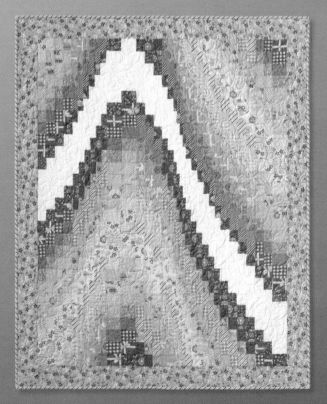

1 cut

From the contrasting fabric, cut:

- (2) 9" strips across the width of the fabric. Remove the selvages. Cut 1 strip in half vertically along the fold. Set 1 of the half strips aside for another project.

2 make strip sets

Arrange the color order of (12) 2½" strips from dark to light. Number the strips from 1 – 12 to keep track of the color order.

NOTE: *As you open the roll of strips, they should already be sorted by color value.*

Sew the strips together along the length. **Make 3** strip sets following the same color order. 2A

Sew a strip set to the top of the contrasting 9" x width of fabric strip. Flip a strip set 180° and sew it to the bottom of the 9" strip, thus reversing the order of the strips. Remove the darkest strip from the top strip set. 2B

Cut the remaining strip set in half vertically. Sew 1 piece to the top of the short contrasting 9" strip using the same color order as before (darkest strip on top and the lightest touching the contrasting fabric). Remove the top (darkest) strip. Turn the remaining half strip set 180° and sew it to the bottom half of the contrasting fabric. 2C

Sew the top of the strip set to the bottom of the strip set with right sides facing to form a tube. Repeat for the smaller strip set. 2D

3 cut and sew

Cut the tubes into the following sizes:

- (3) 3" strips*
- (13) 2" strips*
- (14) 1½" strips*
- (4) 1" strips*

Refer to chart on adjacent page for placement.

Count up from the contrasting fabric to strip #11 and open the seam above the strip. After the seam is opened, press the seam allowances all in one direction. 3A

Count up from the contrasting fabric to strip #10 and open the seam above that strip. Press the seam allowances in the opposite direction as the first. 3B

2C

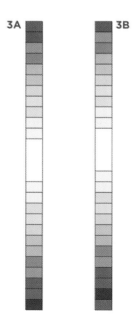

2D

3A   3B

Follow the chart below and continue in this manner, opening the seams and pressing the strips in opposite directions. 3C

Sew the strips together to complete the center of the quilt.

4 border

Cut (6) 4″ strips across the width of the fabric. Sew the strips together end-to-end to make one long strip. Trim the borders from this strip.

Refer to Borders (pg. 110) in the Construction Basics to measure and cut the borders. The strips are approximately 55″ for the sides and approximately 50½″ for the top and bottom.

5 quilt and bind

Layer the quilt with batting and backing and quilt. After the quilting is complete, square up the quilt and trim away all excess batting and backing. Add binding to complete the quilt. See Construction Basics (pg. 110) for binding instructions.

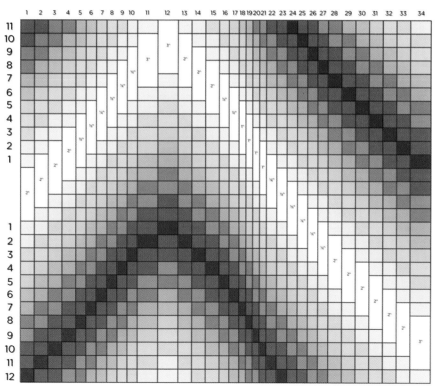

3C

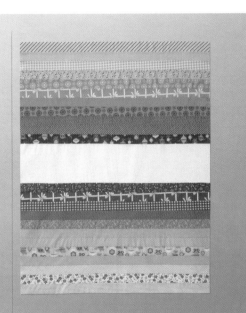

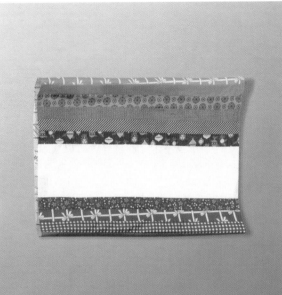

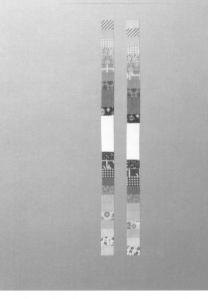

1 Make strip sets. Arrange the color order of (12) 2½″ strips from dark to light. Sew the strips together along the length. Sew a strip set to the top of the 9″ contrasting piece. Flip a strip set 180° and sew it to the bottom of the contrasting strip after removing the darkest strip from the top set.

2 Sew the top of the strip set to the bottom of the second strip set, thus making a tube.

3 Refer to the directions on page 28 and cut the number of strips in the widths given. Count up from the contrasting fabric to strip #11 and open the seam above the strip. For the next strip, count up from the contrasting fabric to strip #10, and open the seam allowance above. Follow the chart and continue cutting strips.

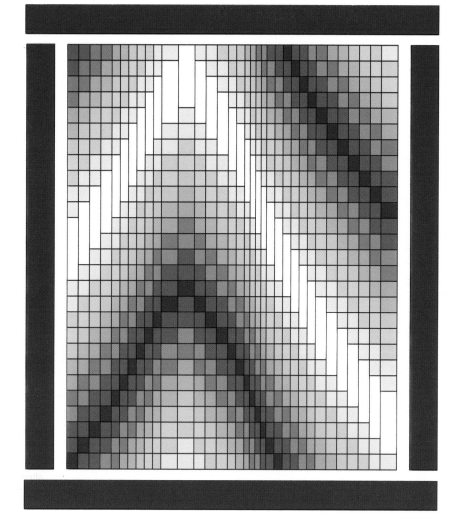

twinkling stars

The first Christmas that Kim and Brad spent as a married couple was destined to be dripping with romance and perfection, right? After all, it had only been two months since they said, "I do," and the twinkle in their lovestruck eyes rivaled the sparkliest strand of Christmas lights. But then it came time to pick out a tree.

Kim grew up with an artificial tree. Every Christmas, it was pulled out of storage, as perky and green as the year before. "It just makes sense," explained Kim. "You buy one tree and it lasts forever. Buying a new tree every year seems like such a waste of money."

Brad grew up with real trees. He couldn't imagine a Christmas season without the fresh scent of pine floating through the house. Besides, he argued, hunting for the perfect tree was always one of best parts of his childhood Christmases.

In the end, it was decided that they would get a real tree, and if Kim wasn't convinced of its superiority, they would buy an artificial tree during the post-holiday clearances.

On a brisk Saturday morning, they hopped into Brad's old red pickup truck and headed to the mountains, turning off the main highway onto a bumpy little road that wound its way up to a beautiful, hilly Christmas tree farm.

The winter thus far had been a mild one, and there was just a light dusting of snow on the ground. The man at the entrance handed Brad an old rusty bow saw and made a sweeping gesture toward the tree covered hills. "Pick yerselfs a good 'un."

They thanked the man and headed out to find their tree. They passed itty bitty baby trees, a few big but oddly-shaped specimens, and dozens and dozens of stumps. As they got further from the gate, they found themselves surrounded by hundreds of evergreens of every shape and size. Off to the left, Kim spotted a beautifully symmetrical tree that was just the right height—and it even had a perfectly straight branch at the top, perfect for Kim's vintage Christmas tree angel.

Brad secured the tree in the bed of the pickup and they headed home to decorate. The next morning, Kim woke up to the intoxicating aroma of fresh evergreen. It smelled like Christmas! She made herself a festive cup of cocoa and wandered over to admire the tree. Suddenly, she saw it—a teeny, tiny spider, scurrying on the wall behind the tree. Then another. And another. The wall was crawling with baby spiders—and they had come from the Christmas tree! Needless to say, Kim and Brad quickly became the proud owners of an artificial tree, and it has served them well for many years—no spiders included!

For the tutorial and everything you need to make this quilt visit:
www.msqc.co/holidayblock18

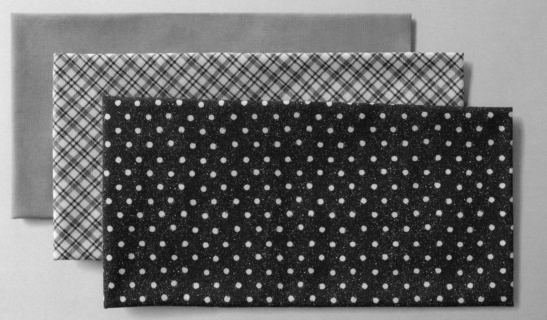

materials

QUILT SIZE
74" x 84"

BLOCK SIZE
8" finished

QUILT TOP
4 packages 5" print squares
3¼ yards solid green background
   fabric - includes sashing and inner
   border

OUTER BORDER
1½ yards

BINDING
¾ yard

BACKING
5¼ yards – vertical seam(s)

SAMPLE QUILT
Overnight Delivery by Sweetwater
for Moda Fabrics

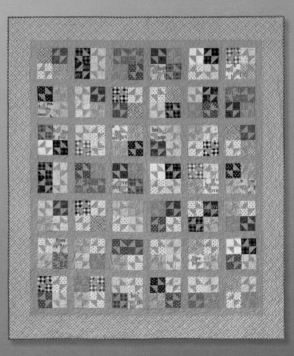

1 cut

From the solid green background fabric, cut:

- (39) 2½" strips across the width of the fabric - subcut 21 strips into 2½" squares. Each strip will yield 16 squares and a **total of 336** are needed.

- 9 strips into 2½" x 8½" rectangles for a **total of 35 vertical sashing rectangles**.

- Subcut 3 strips into 2½" x 20" rectangles. Set aside with the remaining (6) 2½" x width of fabric strips to use when making horizontal sashing strips.

Note: The rest of the yardage will be used for the inner border.

Cut each 5" print square in half vertically and horizontally to make (4) 2½" squares for a **total of 672.**

Stack all matching prints together.

2 mark and sew

On the reverse side of each 2½" background square, draw a line from corner to corner once on the diagonal to mark a sewing line. If you would rather not take the time to draw a line, fold each background square once on the diagonal and press a crease in place to mark the line. **2A**

Select 4 matching 2½" print squares. Layer a marked 2½" background square with a print square. Sew on the marked line, then trim ¼" away from the sewn seam. Open and press the seam allowance toward the darker fabric. **Make 2** matching half-square triangle units. **2B**

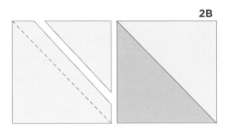

Sew a 2½" matching print square to a half-square triangle unit. **Make 2 rows** and sew the rows together as shown. This makes 1 quadrant of the block. **Make 4 quadrants**. **2C**

Notice that each quadrant is made up of matching prints but the quadrants don't match.

Sew the 4 quadrants together to complete 1 block. **Make 42. 2D**

Block Size: 8" finished

3 arrange and sew

Lay out the blocks in rows. Each row is made up of **6 blocks** and **7 rows** are needed. Sew a 2½" x 8½" sashing rectangle between each block as you sew each row together. After the blocks have been sewn into rows, press the seam allowances of the sashing rectangles toward the blocks.

Make horizontal sashing strips. Trim the selvages off of each strip. Sew a 2½" x 20" strip to one end of a 2½" x width of fabric strip. Measure the row of sewn and sashed blocks. It should measure approximately 58½" across. Trim the strip to your measurement. **Make 6.**

Sew the rows together, adding a horizontal sashing strip between each row to complete the center of the quilt. Press the seam allowances of the sashing strips toward the blocks.

4 inner border

Cut (7) 2½" strips across the width of the fabric. Sew the strips together end-to-end to make one long strip. Trim the borders from this strip.

Refer to Borders (pg. 110) in the Construction Basics to measure and cut the inner borders. The strips are approximately 68½" for the sides and approximately 62½" for the top and bottom.

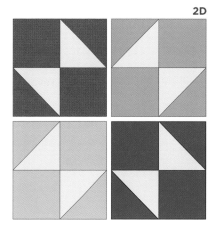

2D

5 outer border

Cut (8) 6½" strips across the width of the fabric. Sew the strips together end-to-end to make one long strip. Trim the borders from this strip.

Refer to Borders (pg. 110) in the Construction Basics to measure and cut the outer borders. The strips are approximately 72½" for the sides and approximately 74½" for the top and bottom.

6 quilt and bind

Layer the quilt with batting and backing and quilt. After the quilting is complete, square up the quilt and trim away all excess batting and backing. Add binding to complete the quilt. See Construction Basics (pg. 110) for binding instructions.

1 Layer a marked 2½″ solid green background square with a 2½″ print square with right sides facing. Sew on the marked line, then trim ¼″ away from the sewn seam. Open and press.

2 Sew a 2½″ matching print square to a half-square triangle unit. Make 2 rows and sew the rows together as shown to make 1 quadrant of the block.

3 Make 4 quadrants and sew them together to complete 1 block.

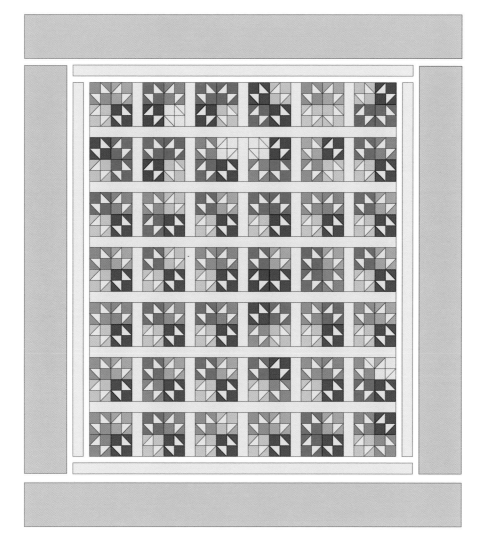

For the tutorial and everything you need to make this quilt visit:
www.msqc.co/holidayblock18

easy half-hexagon

Children all over the world wait with great anticipation for Santa Claus to come visit their homes. In some European countries, they leave out carrots and hay for his reindeer, stuffed into their small shoes in exchange for treats like marzipan, gold coins, and mandarin oranges. In Great Britain and Australia, the children leave mince pies out for Santa. In Sweden, it's a sweet bowl of rice pudding. (I wouldn't mind that myself!) Santa gets a glass of wine from the kids in France, and in Ireland, it's a pint of Guinness! Here in the U.S., the traditional milk and cookies has been a fixture in front of the fireplace for St. Nick since the 1930s. It was given as a symbol of gratitude and a welcome gift when he came down the chimney.

We haven't had little ones in the house for years to set out cookies and milk, with a carrot on the side for Rudolph, but cookies and milk are always a holiday staple in our home! Who knows how many dozens we bake throughout the holiday season, in all their many varieties, from simple sugar cookies with colorful icing and spicy pepparkakor with a delicious, crunchy snap to thumbprints, pinwheels, almond crescents, candy cane cookies, stained glass cookies, gingerbread, shortbread, snowballs, oatmeal kisses, and so many more.

Maybe I'm a bit cookie-obsessed, but I know one little girl who just didn't know when to stop! When Susie's mother made a big batch of her famous wreath cookies, Susie snuck one after the other and hid beneath the table as she finished them off. Soon enough, her mother began to wonder what she was up to. After all, a quiet toddler is not to be trusted! After a quick search, Susie's mother heard quiet crying under the dining room table and found her little girl there, hunched over with green-hued cheeks and lips, staring at her bright green hands with a look of horror on her face. She looked like a little Grinch!

Susie's mother couldn't help but laugh, knowing the culprit was too many cookies that had been tinted green with a bit of food coloring. She explained to Susie that she would be fine, washed her hands up, and warned her to stay away from the cookies for a while. That day, Susie learned an important lesson about moderation, but despite the unwelcome surprise, those irresistible wreath cookies remain her favorite to this day.

WREATH COOKIES

4 cups mini marshmallows
4 cups corn flakes cereal
½ cup salted butter
1 teaspoon green food
  coloring
½ teaspoon vanilla extract
½ cup cinnamon imperials
Waxed paper

Microwave the marshmallows and butter on high for two minutes. Stir. Then, microwave another two minutes and stir until no lumps remain. The butter and marshmallows can also be melted on low heat in a large pot on the stove. Add the green food coloring to the melted marshmallows and quickly mix in the corn flakes. Drop by large spoonfuls onto waxed paper and form into a wreath shape with a hole in the center. Sprinkle a few cinnamon imperials onto each wreath. Let cool. Store in layers with waxed paper in between to prevent sticking. Enjoy!

materials

QUILT SIZE
55⅜" x 72¾"

BLOCK SIZE
4⅛" X 9½" finished

QUILT TOP
1 package 10" print squares

INNER BORDER
½ yard

OUTER BORDER
1¼ yards

BINDING
¾ yard

BACKING
3½ yards – horizontal seam(s)

OTHER
Missouri Star Quilt Co.
10" Half-Hexagon Template

SAMPLE QUILT
Let It Sparkle by RJR Studios for
RJR Fabrics

1A

1B

1 fold and cut

Fold each 10" square in half. Place the template atop a folded square with the short edge aligned with the raw edges of the square. Cut around the template. Each square will yield 2 half-hexagons and a total of 84 are needed. Stack all matching pieces together. **1A 1B**

2 lay out rows

Lay out the half-hexagons in rows. Each row is made using **6 half-hexagons** and every other piece is turned 180°. As you lay out the pieces, make sure the prints match up from one row to the next. Lay out **14 rows**. **2A**

3 sew

Pick up the first half-hexagon in the row you have layed out. Notice that the 2 corners on the long edge are squared off rather than pointed. Place the first piece atop the second with right sides facing. Align the edges of the 2 pieces, then sew the two together. The pointed piece of the second half-hexagon should peek out from behind the squared off edge of the first piece. **3A 3B**

Press the seam allowance toward the darker fabric. **3C**

Continue sewing the half-hexagons together until each row has been completed. Then sew the rows together to complete the center of the quilt.

2A

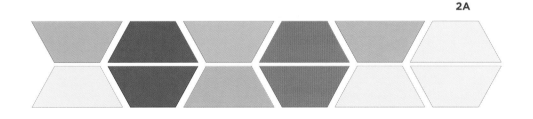

3A

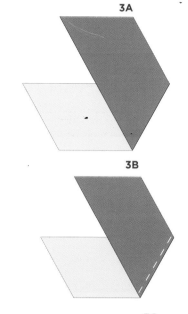

3B

3C

4 trim

Align a ruler with the shortest edges of the blocks along the side of the quilt. Trim off the pointed edges so the side of the quilt is straight. Repeat for the other side.

4A

5 inner border

Cut (6) 2½" strips across the width of the fabric. Sew the strips together end-to-end to make one long strip. Trim the borders from this strip.

Refer to Borders (pg. 110) in the Construction Basics to measure and cut the inner borders. The strips are approximately 57¼" for the sides and approximately 44⅞" for the top and bottom.

4A

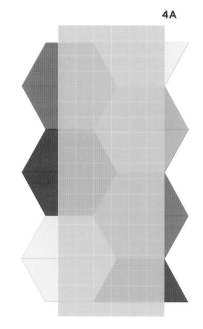

6 outer border

Cut (6) 6" strips across the width of the fabric. Sew the strips together end-to-end to make one long strip. Trim the borders from this strip.

Refer to Borders (pg. 110) in the Construction Basics to measure and cut the outer borders. The strips are approximately 61¼" for the sides and approximately 55⅞" for the top and bottom

7 quilt and bind

Layer the quilt with batting and backing and quilt. After the quilting is complete, square up the quilt and trim away all excess batting and backing. Add binding to complete the quilt. See Construction Basics (pg. 110) for binding instructions.

1 Fold each 10″ square in half. Place the template atop a folded square the short edge aligned with the raw edges of the square. Cut around the template. Stack all matching half-hexagons together.

2 Lay out the half-hexagons in rows. Notice that every other piece is turned 180° and that the prints are matched up from 1 row to the next.

3 Align the short edges of 2 half-hexagons together with right sides facing. Sew the 2 together along the short edges.

4 Press the seam allowance toward the darker fabric.

5 After all rows have been sewn together, place a ruler along the edge and trim away the points.

For the tutorial and everything
you need to make this quilt visit:
www.msqc.co/holidayblock18

josh's star

Call it what you will: White Elephant, Yankee Swap, the Grinch Game, Thieving Elves, or any of its many other names, a gag gift exchange has become a favorite holiday tradition with many of my friends and family. We Doans have a big sense of humor, so you can imagine how it all shakes down when we get to swappin'!

There's a huge mound of gifts in the center of the room, wrapped in everything from plain old newspaper to fancy gift bags, and from tiny to enormous! No matter what you might find inside, it's generally hilarious and gets us cracking jokes. By the end, there's wrapping paper every-which-where, odd gifts scattered throughout the room, and we're out of breath from laughing so hard.

The rules may vary, but we like to play the game like this: Everyone who brought a gift is counted and then that many numbers are written on small slips of paper, folded up, and placed in a bowl. Each participant chooses a random number from a bowl and we sit in order, as best as we can. When it comes time to open a gift, one is chosen from the pile of gifts in the center—which have no identifying gift tags—and it is unwrapped and shown to everyone in the group. That person's turn is over, but the game's just begun!

This is when things get a little more interesting. The next person in line can choose to either "steal" any of the previously unwrapped, available gifts, or choose a new, wrapped gift from the pile. Gifts may be stolen twice.

Once they have been stolen twice, they remain with the third person. So, the first person unwraps the gift, the second person steals the gift, and the third person keeps the gift. The game continues until everyone has taken their turn and all the gifts are unwrapped. A special exception at the end is, the first person who opened a gift may then take one more turn and choose to swap their own gift with any of the available gifts left. And that's how the game's played!

Some of my favorite White Elephant gifts I've ever seen include: a giant, 4 pound can of tuna, a box of Life cereal filled with lemons (get it?), a baggie filled with "donut seeds" a.k.a. Cheerios, two large baguettes carved into "loafers," a jar filled with beans marked "bubble bath," a bottle of water labeled "melted snowman," likewise, a baggie of marshmallows labeled "snowman poop," and a jar of metal nuts labeled "fat-free mixed nuts."

Adding a little humor to the holidays is always welcome, especially during a season with such high expectations. Have fun and try not to take yourself too seriously this year! Whenever I find myself too focused on perfection, I like to remember that it's not what's under the tree that really matters, it's who's around it.

materials

QUILT SIZE
73" x 73"

BLOCK SIZE
18" finished

SUPPLIES
1 package 10" print squares

SASHING AND INNER BORDER
1 yard

OUTER BORDER
1¼ yards

BINDING
¾ yard

BACKING
4½ yards - vertical seam(s)

OTHER
Missouri Star Quilt Co. Large
   Dresden Plate Template

SAMPLE QUILT
Holiday Flourish 11 by Peggy Toole for
Robert Kaufman

1 cut

From the sashing fabric, cut:

- (6) 2½″ strips across the width of the fabric – subcut each of 3 strips into (2) 2½″ x 18½″ rectangles. Set aside until you are ready to sew the quilt top together. Sew the remaining 3 strips together end-to-end and set aside for the horizontal sashing strips. The remaining fabric will be used for the inner border.

2 sew

Select 20 medium to dark print squares.

Layer 2 squares together with right sides facing. Sew on 2 adjacent sides of the squares. **2A**

Measure 5″ in from the outer sewn edge to the center of the sewn squares. Cut in half vertically. Open and press the seam allowance toward the darker fabric. **2B**

Select 20 light to medium/light squares. Sew on 2 adjacent sides of the squares as before. Measure in 5″ from the edge and cut in half vertically. Open and press the

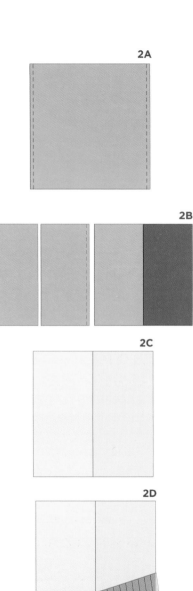

2A

2B

2C

2D

seam allowance toward the darker fabric. **2C**

Align the long edge of the Dresden Plate template along the bottom of a pieced rectangle. Cut along the edge of the template. You will have a two-toned wedge shape. Repeat for all the pieced rectangles. **2D**

Stack the light wedges together and place the darker wedges in another stack.

With right sides facing, sew a light wedge shape to a darker rectangle that has been trimmed. Notice as you align the two pieces that the wedge shape is slightly offset by about ¼″. That's the seam allowance needed so the block will lie flat. You'll need 4 to complete one block. **Make 5 blocks** using light wedges with darker trimmed rectangles. **2E**

Follow the instructions given above, and sew a dark wedge to a lighter trimmed rectangle. You'll need 4 to complete one block.

Make 4 blocks using the darker wedges with the lighter trimmed rectangles. **2F**

Block Size: 18″ finished

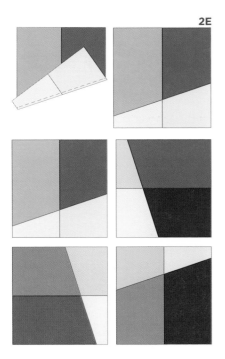

2E

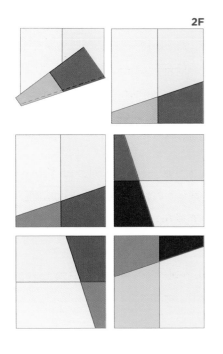

2F

3 arrange and sew

Lay out the blocks in rows. Each row is made up of **3 blocks** across and **3 rows** are needed. Alternate a darker block with a lighter block, adding a vertical sashing rectangle between each block. Refer to the diagram on page 55 for color placement of the blocks. Sew the blocks and sashing strips together into rows. Press the seam allowances toward the sashing rectangles.

Measure the rows. They should be about 58½". From the horizontal sashing strip, trim 2 strips to your measurement. Sew the rows together, adding a horizontal sashing strip between each row.

4 inner border

Cut (7) 2½" strips across the width of the fabric. Sew the strips together end-to-end to make one long strip. Trim the borders from this strip.

Refer to Borders (pg. 110) in the Construction Basics to measure and cut the inner borders. The strips are approximately 58½" for the sides and approximately 62½" for the top and bottom.

5 outer border

Cut (7) 6" strips across the width of the fabric. Sew the strips together end-to-end to make one long strip. Trim the borders from this strip.

Refer to Borders (pg. 110) in the Construction Basics to measure and cut the outer borders. The strips are approximately 62½" for the sides and approximately 73½" for the top and bottom.

6 quilt and bind

Layer the quilt with batting and backing and quilt. After the quilting is complete, square up the quilt and trim away all excess batting and backing. Add binding to complete the quilt. See Construction Basics (pg. 110) for binding instructions.

1 Layer a medium 10″ square with a dark 10″ square with right sides facing. Sew on 2 adjacent sides of the squares using a ¼″ seam allowance.

2 Measure 5″ in from the outer edge of the sewn squares. Cut in half vertically. Open and press the seam allowance toward the darker fabric. Repeat, using light to medium light squares.

3 Align the long edge of the Dresden Plate template along the bottom of a pieced rectangle. Cut along the edge of the template to make a two-toned wedge shape. Repeat for all pieced rectangles.

4 Sew a light wedge to a darker rectangle that has been trimmed. Make 4 quadrants and sew them together to complete one block.

5 Sew a dark wedge to a lighter rectangle that has been trimmed. Make 4 quadrants and sew them together to complete one block.

For the tutorial and everything
you need to make this quilt visit:
www.msqc.co/holidayblock18

rhombus star

I think it's so wonderful that wintertime holidays hold rich meaning for all kinds of people of different backgrounds. I never knew much about Hanukkah growing up, but I've always loved the beautiful blue and silver decorations, the Star of David, and of course the many glowing lights I see in Hanukkah decor. As I've come to know more people who celebrate Hanukkah, I think I understand better the special meanings behind this beautiful holiday.

Hanukkah, or the Festival of Lights, is observed every year on the Hebrew calendar date of 25 Kislev, which always falls somewhere between the end of November and the end of December. Sarah Agustina, one of our Missouri Star Quilt Co. photographers, grew up celebrating this wonderful eight-day holiday with her family.

Sarah, her two sisters, and her parents always took turns lighting the candles of the menorah. On the first night, the center candle, or shamash, was lit along with one of the eight side candles. Sarah's father would recount the victory of the Maccabees, the rededication of the temple, and the miracle of the oil.

On the second night, the shamash and two other candles were lit. This continued, with one additional candle being lit each night until the final night, when all nine candles were lit at once. Every night was highlighted with yummy foods and fun little gifts like toys, gift cards, or Hanukkah-themed movies that they could watch together during the celebration.

Sarah's mother fried potato pancakes called latkes in oil to represent the miracle of the oil so many years ago. The latkes were served with the traditional side of applesauce, and then it was time for a game of dreidel. A dreidel is a four-sided spinning top with Hebrew symbols on each side. They used chocolate coins as betting tokens, which were won or lost with the spin of the top. (Of course, when Sarah and her sisters were very young, her parents often let them win even when they had an unlucky spin!)

I love learning about the holiday traditions of my friends and neighbors. Year after year, those traditions stitch our hearts to past generations like the pieces of one, big family quilt.

materials

QUILT SIZE
69½ x 90"

BLOCK SIZE
18½" X 20½" finished

QUILT TOP
1¾ yards white fabric
3¼ yards background fabric
    – includes inner border

OUTER BORDER
1½ yards

BINDING
¾ yard

BACKING
5½ yards – vertical seam(s)

OTHER
Missouri Star Quilt Co. 10" Rhombus Template

SAMPLE QUILT
Kona Cotton White Yardage by RK Studios for
Robert Kaufman Lava Sea Batik by Anthology
Fabrics and Essex Linen - Yarn Dyed Oyster
Metallic designed by Robert Kaufman for Robert
Kaufman Fabrics

NOTE: *The fabrics for this quilt may also be switched out for red
and green to make a Christmas Rhombus Star.*

1 cut

From the white fabric, cut:

- (12) 5″ strips across the width of the fabric – subcut each strip into 6 rhombus shapes using the 10″ Rhombus template. You will need 6 rhombus shapes for each star and there are 12 stars used in the quilt. **1A**

From the background fabric, cut:

- (15) 5″ strips across the width of the fabric. Using the 10″ Rhombus template, cut 11 triangles from each strip for a **total of 160.** Rotate the template 180-degrees with each cut to make the most of your fabric. **1B**

Set the remainder of the background fabric aside for the inner border.

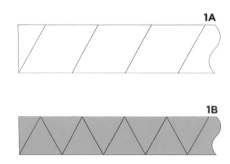

2 block construction

Sew a background triangle to both sides of 1 point of the rhombus to make each star point unit. **Make 6.** 2A

NOTE: *Pressing after each piece is added cuts down on bulk and helps the quilt lie flat.*

Sew 3 star points together to make one half of the block. **Make 2** halves for each star. 2B & 2C

NOTE: *To avoid using any set-in seams, we will be sewing the half blocks into rows, being careful to lay out the quilt so the half blocks become complete stars.*

3 arrange and sew

Lay out the blocks in rows. Be careful to pair each half block with another. Each row is made up of **3 half blocks** and **8 rows** are needed. Sew the blocks together when you are satisfied with the arrangement and add a background triangle to both ends of each row. 3A

Press the seam allowances of the odd-numbered rows toward the right and the even-numbered rows toward the left to make the seams "nest."

Sew the rows together. Trim each side to make the edges straight, leaving ¼″ seam allowance. 3B

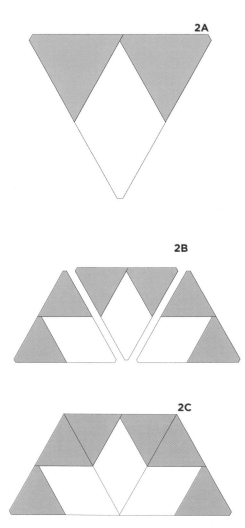

2A

2B

2C

3A

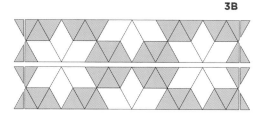

3B

4 inner border

Cut (4) 6″ strips across the width of the fabric. Sew the strips together end-to-end to make one long strip. Trim the 2 side borders from this strip. Each strip should measure approximately 74½″. Refer to Borders (pg. 110) in the Construction Basics to learn how to measure and cut the borders to the correct size.

Cut (3) 2½″ strips across the width of the fabric. Sew the strips together end-to-end to make one long strip. Trim the top and bottom borders from this strip. Each strip will measure approximately 58″. Refer to Borders (pg. 110) in the Constructions Basics to learn how to measure and cut the borders to the correct size.

5 outer border

Cut (7) 6½″ strips across the width of the fabric. Sew the strips together end-to-end to make one long strip. Trim the borders from this strip.

Refer to Borders (pg. 110) in the Construction Basics to measure and cut the outer borders. The strips are approximately 78½″ for the sides and approximately 70″ for the top and bottom.

6 quilt and bind

Layer the quilt with batting and backing and quilt. After the quilting is complete, square up the quilt and trim away all excess batting and backing. Add binding to complete the quilt. See Construction Basics (pg. 110) for binding instructions.

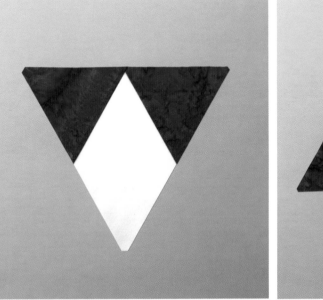

1 Sew a blue background triangle to both sides of 1 point of a white rhombus to make each star point unit.

2 Sew 3 star points together to make one half of the block. Make 2 halves for each star and leave the 2 halves separate until the quilt has been laid out.

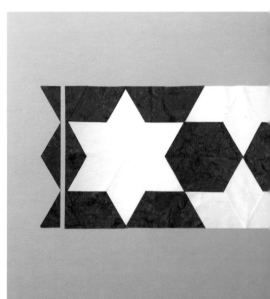

3 After the quilt top has been completed, trim each side to make the edges straight. Be sure to leave a ¼" seam allowance at the end of each star point.

For the tutorial and everything you need to make this quilt visit:
www.msqc.co/holidayblock18

fence rail stars

It's easy to go along in life, as happy as a bug in a rug, without getting too worried about the bigger perspective. Days blur together and I often get caught up in all the little things that keep me busy, until I encounter an obstacle that makes me stop and think about where I really am and what's most important. In those moments, it's easy to panic and think about all my future plans all at once, or, if I'm in the right state of mind, I stop to appreciate where I've been and focus my efforts on the next step. All we ever really need is just one step ahead.

My friend Sherry recently told me a story about trying to take her family out to a pumpkin patch, and it immediately reminded me of those moments in life that make me pause and reflect. They had decided to go out together one autumn night and take the kids to pick out their pumpkins, but as soon as those kids caught a glimpse of the brightly painted corn maze sign, they couldn't be swayed. They had to go inside and check it out!

Without knowing what they'd done, this innocent little family had stepped inside one of the most challenging corn mazes in their state! As they journeyed further in, the lights and sounds of the surrounding farm faded and the ground turned to mud. The kids splashed in puddles and ducked into stands of corn to scare each other, but after a while, the fun wore off and they realized they were truly lost.

An hour into their time in the maze, they stopped to regroup and decide what to do. It was getting darker, the kids were complaining, and Sherry just kept shaking her head, trying her best not to utter an "I told you so." Her husband munched happily on a giant bag of kettle corn, seemingly oblivious to their plight. He continued to crunch away as they discussed what they should do, when Sherry abruptly grabbed his bag of popcorn.

She quickly explained her plan to her husband and the kids and they all agreed. They kept retracing steps, so they had to use some kind of marker to know where they'd been. Sherry's idea for their escape took a page right out of Hansel and Gretel: As they progressed through the maze, they dropped pieces of popcorn every couple of feet to mark their path. To her husband's disbelief (and hunger), they soon found their way out!

The bag of popcorn had been depleted, they were dirty and tired, but they were triumphant! They'd never been so happy to sit together on hay bales and have donuts and cider. So, in the end, she realized it had actually been a successful family outing after all. Being lost brought them together and made them work as a team. Despite muddy shoes, they all left the farm smiling, and with bright orange pumpkins held tightly in their arms.

materials

QUILT SIZE
43" X 43"

BLOCK SIZE
18" finished

SUPPLY LIST
1 roll of 2½" strips
1 yard background fabric – includes
  border

BINDING
½ yard

BACKING
3 yards - vertical seam(s)

SAMPLE QUILT
Pumpkin Patch Batik by Kathy Engle
for Island Batiks

Note: *There are enough strips to make two
small quilts. If you choose to do so, double the
amount of background fabric. Or if you prefer,
you can set the remaining fabric aside for
another project.*

fence rail stars quilt

1 cut

From the background fabric, cut:

- (4) 4" strips across the width
  of the fabric. Subcut 3 strips
  into 4" squares. Each strip
  will yield 10 squares for a **total
  of 30.** Cut (2) 4" squares from
  the remaining strip.

2 sew

Make strip sets by sewing (3) 2½" print
strips together along the length. **Make 6**
and cut (6) 6½" squares from each strip
set for a **total of 36** squares. **2A**

3 prepare

On the reverse side of each 4" background
square, draw a line from corner to corner
once on the diagonal. **3B**

4 snowball corners

Place a marked 4" square atop a strip-
pieced square with right sides facing and
the top and side edges aligned. **4A**

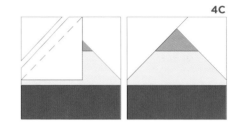

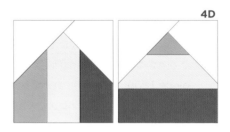

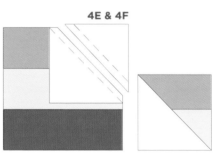

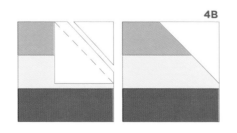

Sew on the line. Trim ¼" away from the sewn seam, open and press the seam allowance toward the strip-pieced square. **4B**

Repeat for the adjacent side of the square. **4C**

Make 2 units with the strips running horizontally and 2 units with the strips running vertically. **4D**

Note: It's easy to make some extra half-square triangles in the process of snowballing the corners of the strip-pieced squares. Just sew another seam ½" from the first and cut between the sewn seams. Open the smaller half-square triangle and press the seam allowance toward the darker fabric. Toss them in a box and use when needed! **4E & 4F**

5 block construction

Sew a strip-pieced square to either side of a snowballed square. Be aware of the direction the strips run. **Make 2 rows. 5A**

Sew a snowballed square to either side of a strip-pieced square. **Make 1 row** in this manner. **5B**

Sew the three rows together to complete 1 block. **Make 4. 5C**

Block Size: 18" finished

6 arrange and sew

Sew the blocks together in a 4-patch arrangement. Notice 2 blocks have been turned and the strips run vertically in the center patch in the block in the upper right and lower left. **5D**

7 border

Cut (4) 4" strips across the width of the fabric. Sew the strips together end-to-end to make one long strip. Trim the borders from this strip.

Refer to Borders (pg. 110) in the Construction Basics to measure and cut the borders. The strips are approximately 36½" for the sides and approximately 43½" for the top and bottom.

8 quilt and bind

Layer the quilt with batting and backing and quilt. After the quilting is complete, square up the quilt and trim away all excess batting and backing. Add binding to complete the quilt. See Construction Basics (pg. 110) for binding instructions.

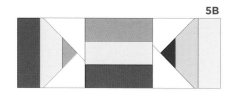

5B

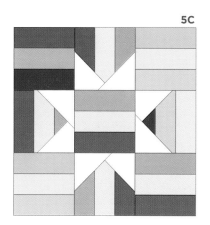

5C

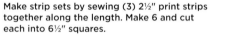

1 Make strip sets by sewing (3) 2½″ print strips together along the length. Make 6 and cut each into 6½″ squares.

2 Place a marked 4½″ square atop a strip-pieced square with right sides facing. Sew on the marked line, then trim the excess fabric away ¼″ from the sewn seam.

3 Place a marked 4½″ square on the adjacent side of the square. Sew on the marked line, then trim the excess fabric away as before. Open and press.

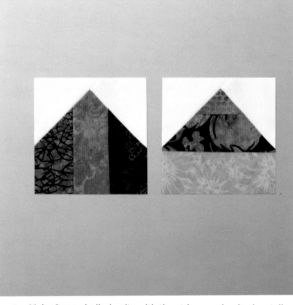

4 Make 2 snowballed units with the strips running horizontally and 2 with the strips running vertically.

5 Sew a strip-pieced square to either side of a snowballed square to make the first and third row. Sew a snowballed square to either side of a strip-pieced square to make the center row. Be aware of the direction the strips are running in each row.

fall shenanigans

When fall comes around, I can't help but crave a sweet slice of pumpkin pie—smooth and custardy, on a flaky crust with a generous dollop of whipped cream. I could eat it for breakfast, lunch, or dinner, and sometimes I do! It's incredible to me that this delicious treat comes from such an odd-looking squash. Whoever thought to take a pumpkin and turn it into a pie was definitely a genius, or at least very hungry.

While most of us only think about pumpkins when it comes time to carve a jack-'o-lantern or bake a pie, there are some people who are obsessed with pumpkins. They think about growing them all year long, with incredible results! Last year, a Belgian man named Mathis Willemijns set the world record with a pumpkin weighing 2,222 pounds. The previous year, he'd gone even bigger with a behemoth weighing 2,625 pounds, well over a ton on both! He admits that his hobby of growing pumpkins had perhaps gotten out of hand. I might be able to say the same about one of my hobbies too.

You might wonder: what happens to those record-setting pumpkins when the contest is over? In most cases, they're cut into smaller pieces and fed to animals, but just imagine if you made them into pies. You only need about 1-2 pounds of pumpkin to make a pie, so one of those giants could make over 1,000 pies! For the folks in New Bremen, Ohio, this wouldn't be a stretch. In 2010, they made the largest pumpkin pie in the world, weighing 3,699 pounds!

Native to Central America, pumpkins are now grown all over the world in many different colors, shapes, and sizes. Some are ghostly white, some are bright red or deep green, and some have smooth skin or warty, knobbly skin. And they're not vegetables, contrary to common belief, they're actually fruits! I personally like to scoop out all the seeds and roast them with salt and pepper in a little olive oil for an easy quilting snack. I keep them right next to my machine and munch away.

The history books might have us believe that the Pilgrims and Native Americans served pumpkin pie at the first Thanksgiving, but it was more likely that they simply ate it as a pumpkin mash or soup, along with roasted turkey, duck, geese, venison, ham, lobster, and clams. Pair that with a side of berries, fruit, and squash, and you'd have an authentic meal. Myself, I'm happy to have my pumpkin in a pie, right alongside some ice cream.

For the tutorial and everything
you need to make this quilt visit:
www.msqc.co/holidayblock18

materials

QUILT SIZE
40½" x 40"

SUPPLIES
1 package 10" print squares
 - we used Halloween-themed fabric

½ yard background

BORDER
½ yard

BINDING
½ yard

BACKING
2½ yards - vertical seam(s)

OTHER
(1) 4½" x 6½" scrap of fusible
 – we used lightweight Heat 'n Bond

Missouri Star Quilt Co. Large Simple
Wedge Template

SAMPLE QUILT
Spook-tacular Hues for Wilmington
Prints

Because there are different elements to make for this quilt, we thought it might be easiest to "cut as we go" when making each section.

Section 1 - Cats

Select (6) 10" squares, 3 to use as cats and 3 for background.

1 cut

From each of the 3 squares being used for cats, cut:

- (2) 5" x 10" rectangles – trim
  1 rectangle to 5" x 9½" – subcut
  the other rectangle into (1)
  3" x 5" rectangle and (1)
  2½" x 5" rectangle. Cut the
  2½" rectangle into (2) 2½"
  squares. Set aside the remaining
  4½" x 5" rectangle for another
  project. Keep all matching
  prints stacked together.

From each of the squares being used as background for the cats, cut:

- (1) 5" square, (1) 2½" x 5"
  rectangle, and (1) 2½" square.
  Set the remaining fabric aside
  for another project.

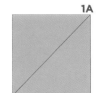

1A

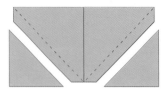

1B

1C

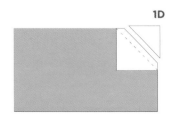

1D

1E

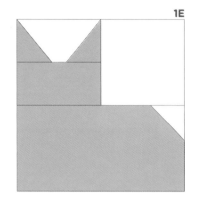

2 sew

Fold 2 matching 2½" squares from corner to corner once on the diagonal. The fold line marks your sewing line. Place a square on each end of a 2½" x 5" background rectangle with right sides facing. Sew along the crease, then trim the excess fabric ¼" away from the sewn seam. **1A**

Add a matching 3" x 5" rectangle to complete the cat's head. **1B**

Sew the cat's head to the left side of a background 5" square. **1C**

Pick up the matching 5" x 9½" print rectangle. Fold a crease from corner to corner once on the diagonal of the background 2½" square. Place the square on the upper right corner of the print rectangle with right sides facing. Sew along the crease, then trim the excess fabric ¼" away from the sewn seam. Open and press the seam toward the print fabric. **1D**

Sew the two portions together to complete one cat block. **Make 3** and sew them together in a horizontal row. **1E**

Block Size: 9" finished

Section 2 – Pumpkin

1 cut

From the background fabric, cut:

- (1) 10" square – subcut the square in half horizontally and vertically to make (4) 5" squares for a **total of 4.**

- (1) 6¼" x 27½" rectangle

- (1) 2¾" x 27½" rectangle

- (1) 2¾" strip across the width of the fabric – subcut the strip into (2) 2¾" x 18½" rectangles.

Select (5) 10" squares. Cut each square in half horizontally and vertically to make (4) 5" squares for a **total of 20.**

Trace the pumpkin stem found on this page onto the paper side of the fusible. Roughly cut around the stem and press to the reverse side of a contrasting print square. Cut out the stem and set it aside until the pumpkin section is sewn together.

2 sew

Sew (5) 5" squares together into a row. **Make 4 rows.** Press the even-numbered rows toward the left and the odd-numbered rows toward the right so the seams will "nest." Sew the rows together. **2A**

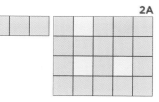
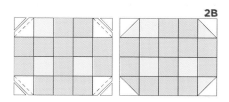

Draw a line from corner to corner once on the diagonal on the reverse side of each of the (4) 5" background squares to mark a sewing line. If you would rather, you can mark your sewing line by folding each square on the diagonal and pressing a crease in place. Place a marked square on each outer corner of the sewn rows of squares. Sew on the marked line, then trim ¼" away from the sewn seam. After the corners have been snowballed, open and press the seam allowances toward the pumpkin. **2B**

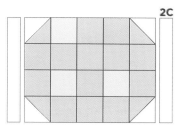

Sew a 2¾" x 18½" background rectangle to both sides of the pumpkin. Press the seam allowances toward the pumpkin. **2C**

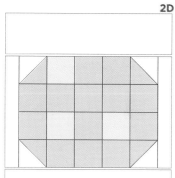

Sew a 2¾" x 27½" background rectangle to the bottom of the pumpkin and a 6¼" x 27½" background rectangle to the top. Press the seams toward the pumpkin. **2D**

Center the pumpkin stem atop the center square in the top row of the pumpkin. Fuse in place, then stitch around the stem using a blanket stitch. **2E**

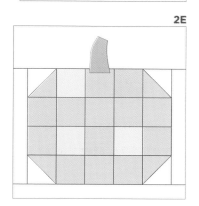

Block Size: 27" x 26" finished

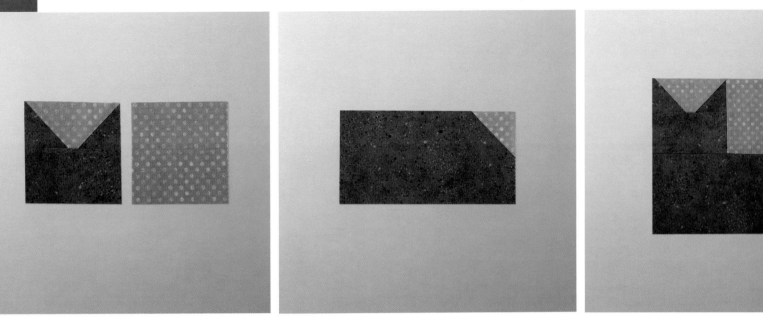

1 Snowball each end of a 2½" x 5" background rectangle using 2½" squares. Sew the snowballed rectangle to a matching 3" x 5" rectangle to make the cat's head. Sew the cat's head to a 5" background square.

2 Using a 2½" square, snowball a matching 5" x 9½" rectangle to make the body of the cat.

3 Sew the top portion of the cat to the body to complete 1 cat.

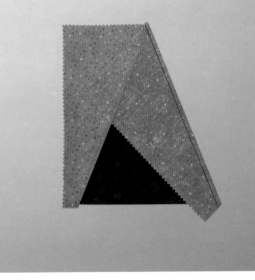

4 Layer (2) 10" squares with right sides facing. Trim 1" off the bottom and set the strips aside. Center the simple wedge template on the layered pieces and cut through both layers on each side of the template.

5 Sew a background side piece to either side of the center triangle.

6 Stitch the 1" strip that was trimmed off previously to the bottom of the piece to complete the hat block.

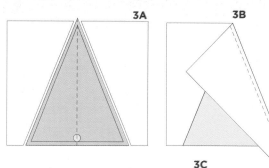

3A

3B

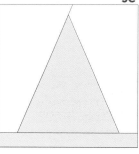

3C

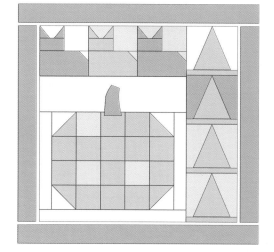

Section 3 – Hats

Select (8) 10" squares – 4 light for the background pieces and 4 dark for the prints.

1 cut

Layer a light background square with a dark square with right sides facing. Trim 1" off the bottom of the layered squares. Set the 1" strip aside as that will become the brim of the hat.

Mark the center of the top layered square along the top edge of the piece with a pencil or by making a crease with your fingernail. Center the simple wedge template on the layered pieces and align the bottom of the template with the bottom on the layered squares. Notice the top of the template extends a little bit above the top edge. Cut through both layers of fabric on each side of the template. **3A**

2 sew

Pick up the background side pieces and sew one to either side of the print triangle. Sew the 1" x 10" print strip to the bottom and trim to fit. **Make 4 hats. 3B, 3C**

Block Size: 8½" x 8¾" finished

Note: you have enough pieces left to make another hat, if you choose to use them. The colors would be reversed, so the hat would be made using the background fabric and the hat backgrounds would be made using prints.

Sew the hats together in a vertical row.

3 putting it all together

Sew the row of cats to the top of the pumpkin section. Add the row of hats to the right side of the pumpkin/cat section. Refer to the diagram to the left if necessary.

4 border

Cut (4) 3" strips across the width of the fabric. Sew the strips together end-to-end to make one long strip. Trim the borders from this strip.

Refer to Borders (pg. 110) in the Construction Basics to measure and cut the outer borders. The strips are approximately 35½" for the sides and approximately 41" for the top and bottom.

5 quilt and bind

Layer the quilt with batting and backing and quilt. After the quilting is complete, square up the quilt and trim away all excess batting and backing. Add binding to complete the quilt. See Construction Basics (pg. 110) for binding instructions.

For the tutorial and everything you need to make this quilt visit:
www.msqc.co/holidayblock18

grandmother's fan

When Spencer Maddox was three years old, he knew exactly who he wanted to be for Halloween. No, it wasn't Spiderman or Lightning McQueen, it was professional soccer goalkeeper Nick Rimando.

Chances are, you've never heard of Nick Rimando. Chances are you've never heard of a single player on his team, Real Salt Lake. But to this little boy with bright blue eyes and golden curls, Nick Rimando was the epitome of cool.

The shops in Spencer's hometown were bursting with costumes of all types: monsters and witches, ninja turtles and transformers. There were, however, no Nick Rimando costumes. So Spencer's mom went to work.

She found a long sleeve black T-shirt that resembled Rimando's favorite black uniform. Then, she pulled out a bit of white yardage and a roll of fusible interfacing. Carefully, she cut out numbers and letters to applique "Rimando" and a big number eighteen on the back of that shirt.

An old, flat soccer ball was cut open and transformed into a candy basket for trick or treating, and Spencer's arms were covered in temporary tattoos to imitate Rimando's real-life tattooed arms. Spencer put on his makeshift uniform and pushed up the sleeves—just like Nick. He grabbed his soccer ball "basket" and headed out to trick or treat with his cousins.

House after house, the neighbors were delighted by "Darth Vader" Davey and "Elsa" Jane, but no one recognized the little soccer player with the tattooed arms. Of course, Spencer didn't notice. He spent the evening on cloud nine, and when it came time for a bath, he was careful to hold his arms up out of the water to keep the tattoos safe!

Halloween is such a fun time to let your creativity shine. With just a few basic supplies, a simple T-shirt can become anything under the sun! When my friend, Katie, was eight and a half months pregnant, she put on a pair of red pants and stuck colorful round stickers all over her big, round belly and went to a Halloween party as a gumball machine. Another friend went as as a Christmas tree—complete with presents! He dressed all in green and wrapped himself in tinsel and a strand of multi-colored lights. His "shoes" were tissue boxes wrapped up in holiday paper, bows, and gift tags. Of course, he finished off the look with a big, gold star taped to his hat.

One of our cute shop assistants, Kimber Wilson, loves to plan coordinating costumes for her entire family. When she was four years old, everyone—including three giant Newfoundlands and five happy mutts—dressed up as pumpkins. It was so fun, Kimber and her family have continued the tradition of a group costume every year since! They love to sew their own costumes, and they are so talented and creative, we can't wait to see what they'll come up with next!

Why not use this Halloween as an opportunity to let your creativity run wild? Whether it's a table runner, a wall hanging, or a unique costume, create something to make the holiday special!

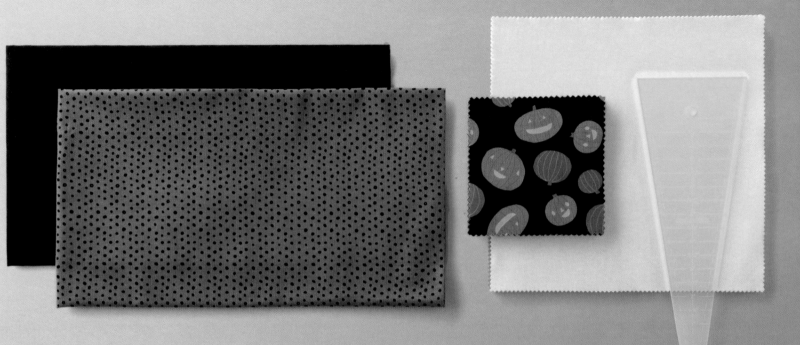

materials

QUILT SIZE
66" X 75½"

BLOCK SIZE
9½" finished

QUILT TOP
3 packages 5" print squares
1 package 42 ct. 10" background
    squares

BORDER
1½ yard – includes fabric for
    quarter circles at base of fans

BINDING
¾ yard

BACKING
4¾ yards – vertical seam(s)

ADDITIONAL SUPPLIES
Missouri Star Quilt Co. Dresden
    Plate Template

SAMPLE QUILT
Cats, Bats, and Jacks by My Mind's
Eye for Riley Blake Designs

1 cut

From the border fabric, cut:

- (2) 5" strips across the width of the fabric. Subcut (8) 5" squares from one strip and (3) 5" squares from the other. Put the rest of the strip aside to use in the outer border. Use the template on (pg. 85) and cut a circle from each 5" background square. Fold each circle in half twice, once vertically, once horizontally. Cut along the fold lines to make quarter circles. Set aside for the moment. 1A

From the 5" print squares, cut:

- 210 fan blades. Align the 5" mark on the template with the top of a 5" square. Cut 1 blade then flip the template 180 degrees and cut a second blade. Each 5" square will yield 2 blades. 1B

NOTE: *You will have some squares left over. Set them aside for another project.*

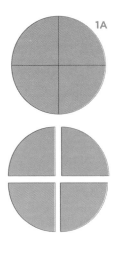

1A

1B

2 sew

Sew 5 blades together to make a fan. **Make 42. 2A**

3 appliqué

Using a small blanket stitch or zigzag, appliqué a fan to one corner of a 10" background square. Place a quarter circle on the corner, covering up the raw ends of the blades. Appliqué in place to complete the block. 3A

Block Size: 9½" Finished

4 lay out blocks

Follow the diagram on (pg. 87) and lay out the blocks in rows. Notice how the blocks are oriented. Each row is made up of **6 blocks** and there are **7 rows.**

When you are satisfied with the arrangement, sew the blocks into rows. Then sew the rows together to complete the center of the quilt top.

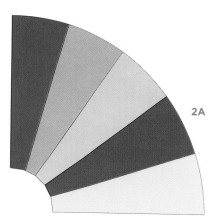

2A

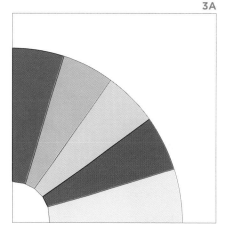

3A

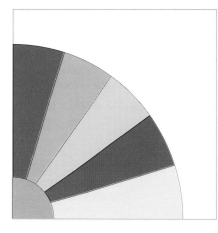

5 border

Cut (7) 5″ strips across the width of the fabric. Sew the strips together end-to-end, adding in the remainder of the strip that was cut to make 5″ squares. Make one long strip and trim the borders from it.

Refer to Borders (pg. 110) in the Construction Basics to measure and cut the outer borders. The strips are approximately 67″ for the sides and approximately 66½″ for the top and bottom.

6 quilt and bind

Layer the quilt with batting and backing and quilt. After the quilting is complete, square up the quilt and trim away all excess batting and backing. Add binding to complete the quilt. See Construction Basics (pg. 110) for binding instructions.

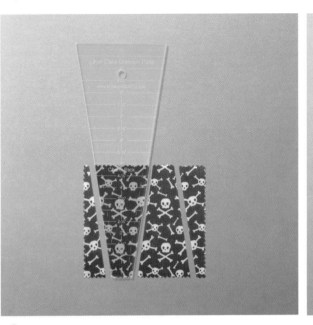

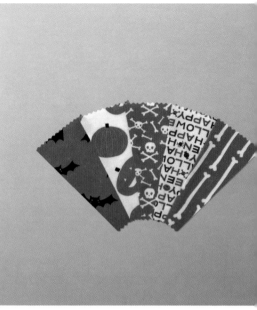

1 Cut circles using the template found on page 85. Fold each circle in half twice, once vertically, once horizontally. Cut along the fold lines to make quarter circles.

2 Align the 5″ mark on the Dresden Plate template with the top of a 5″ square. Cut 1 blade, then flip the template 180° and cut a second blade.

3 Sew 5 blades together to make a fan.

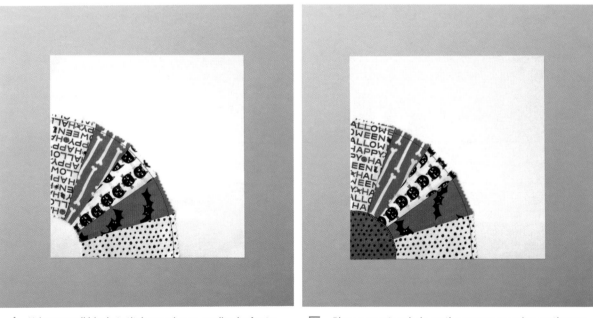

4 Using a small blanket stitch or a zigzag, appliqué a fan to one corner of a 10″ background square.

5 Place a quarter circle on the corner, covering up the raw ends of the blades. Appliqué in place to complete the block.

deck the halls

five handmade gifts for any occasion

These versatile projects make beautiful holiday decorations and excellent last-minute gifts. Grab a stack of your favorite themed prints and create something for every season! No matter what you celebrate, make them your own and have fun!

I adore homemade decorations and when the kids were growing up, the walls of our house were always plastered with their handiwork whether it was winter, spring, summer, or fall. Now that they're grown up, the task has gone to my grandchildren, who definitely keep my fridge covered in their creative pursuits. We all love decorating for holidays and it's fun to add a personal touch to each one with handmade items that can easily be adapted with a variety of seasonal fabrics. It's a great way to complement existing decor and cozy up the place.

A custom wreath can be made up in a variety of fabrics for any and every season. It's such a nice way to welcome guests at your front door. Banners are a lot of fun too! There are so many preprinted panels out there that would make wonderful wall hangings to set the scene in your home, plus they come together in an afternoon!

These projects also double as great last-minute gifts. It's not always possible to stitch up a quilt by the time December rolls around, but a cuddly blipper will definitely keep the chills at bay! And for the techie in the family, try a tablet holder. They'll love toting around their technology in style! From festive wreaths to banners, and cute aprons, we've got something everyone will love.

cut the apron strings

This pattern is used with permission from Patricia Wilkenson of Quilt 'Till you Wilt.

size: Approximately 20" x 35"

supplies
1 yard of fabric
½ - 1 cup plastic pellets
embellishments of your choice

---

mark, cut, and sew

Fold the fabric with right sides together and trim away the selvages. Align a rotary cutting ruler along the fold and trim just enough to straighten the fabric on the top and bottom edges.

Fold the fabric in half again. Measure 4½" in from 1 side and 8" down from the top. Mark the measurements as you go.

Cut the neckline by cutting through all 4 layers of fabric beginning at the 4½" mark, gently curving toward and ending at the 8" mark.

Open the last fold you made.

Note: if you want to add "fidget" ribbons, see instructions at the bottom of the second column as they will need to be added before the apron pieces are stitched together. You will want the raw edges to be enclosed so it remains reversible. Stitch around all edges using a ¼" seam allowance. Leave a 6" opening along the bottom edge.

Turn right side out and top stitch. Be sure to leave the opening along the bottom.

Pour ¼ – ½ cup of plastic pellets into 1 shoulder through the bottom opening. Gathering up the fabric in your hands will help form a little pocket in the shoulder area. After the pellets have been added, sew across that area twice.

Note: using a pencil or a slim, short dowel between the area with the pellets and the sewing machine foot will keep the pellets in place while you stitch.

Repeat for the other shoulder area.

Turn the edges of the bottom opening in toward the inside of the apron. Top-stitch the opening closed.

If you choose to add "fidget" ribbons to the bottom of the apron, you'll need about 1½ yards of ribbon or wide rickrack. We cut 9 pieces of rickrack into 6" increments, folded each piece in half, then basted the raw edges to the bottom of the apron before sewing it closed.

pennant banner

size: 12 feet

supplies
(14) 10" squares
¾" twill tape

---

cut & sew

Fold each 10" square once on the diagonal with right sides facing. Sew down one side.

When you have finished stitching, clip the points off of the sewn end to reduce bulk.

Turn each of the pieces right side out. Use a blunt stiletto or the handle of an artist's paintbrush to push the point out so it looks sharp.

Align the seam allowance with the center point of the top of the piece. Press.

Fold the top down and press.

To attach the pennants to the twill tape, open the flap at the top of the piece. Place the twill tape along the pressed fold. **5A** Fold the flap back down, and stitch across the flap. **5B**

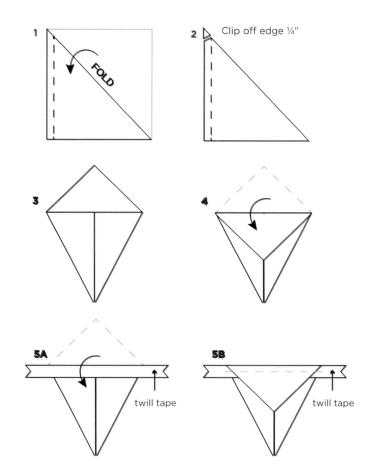

ipad holder

This fun project makes going hands-free easy as can be! It's basically an oversized bean bag to hold your tablet in place while you watch your favorite shows, surf the internet, listen to music, and more! Stitch it up in a favorite print and it makes a great gift for the techie in your family. Check out Rob Appell's original Cell Phone Plop tutorial at http://msqc.co/plop.

size: Approximately 6" x 7"

supplies
½ yard fabric or ¼ yard each of 2 contrasting fabrics
10 - 12 cups filler – rice, beans, lentils or crushed walnut shells (sold in the pet store as lizard litter)

---

cut
(1) 5½" x 24½" rectangle

2 pieces using the template found on this page. Fold the fabric with wrong sides together before pinning and cutting.

sew
Make a mark ¼" away from each end of the rectangle on both sides. Align one mark with one of the points on one of the fabric pieces with right sides facing. Pin the rectangle all around the piece, making sure the mark on each end butts up against the other.

Sew the strip in place beginning and ending the stitches at the marks. You should have ¼" of fabric left unsewn on each end that will be used as the seam allowance when closing the bag.

Note: if your strip is a little longer than necessary, just trim to fit after both sides have been sewn in place.

Align the other side with the strip beginning at the same point as before. Pin and stitch just like you did the other side.

Find the opening where the two ends of the strip meet and sew it closed about 1" – 1½" in from either side of the outer edge. There should be an opening left that is 2" – 3" wide.

Turn the holder right side out. Smooth out the seams with a point turner or your fingers, whichever works best.

Insert a funnel into the opening. Using the filling of your choice, fill the bag. We used 10 - 12 cups of filler.

After filling the bag, whipstitch the opening closed.

blipper

Size: *Approximately 57" x 72" (Adult)*
Size: *Approximately 57" x 56" (Child)*

supplies

Note: *The size of the Blipper depends on the width of the fleece fabric. It is usually 58" – 60" wide, depending on the manufacturer.*

Adult: 2½ yards each of 2 contrasting colors of fleece.
Child: 2 yards each of 2 contrasting colors of fleece.

The Blipper is made using the same instructions no matter which size is being made. If you're sewing for tall people, you might want to measure their height and add some length to your Blipper.

trim

Trim the selvages off of both sides of the fabric. Also, make sure the fabric is cut straight across the top and the bottom of the yardage.

layer and sew

Layer the two pieces of fabric together with right sides facing. Make sure the "nap"* of both pieces are oriented in the same direction. Pin the pieces together to keep them from stretching out of shape.

Sew all the way around the outer edge using a ⅜" - ½" seam allowance. Leave a large enough area unsewn to turn the piece right side out, about 5". Take a few back stitches at the beginning and end of the seam.

Turn the piece right side out. Stitch the open area closed by turning in the edges and top stitching. If you choose, top stitch around the whole piece about ¼" – ½" from the outer edge.

Measure 16" - 18" from the bottom of the piece. Turn up the end and top stitch on both sides, thus making a pocket. Be sure to back stitch at the beginning and end of the seams. **2A**

And you're done! You're all ready to tuck your feet into that pocket and snuggle into the warmth!

nap – The natural direction of the surface texture of the fabric.

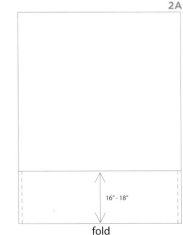

2A

16" - 18"

fold

easy holiday wreaths

size: Approximately 10"

supplies
1 package 10" print squares – use holiday print of your choice
(1) 10" styrofoam wreath form
1 chopstick
Option for fabric: ¾ yard each of 3 different fabrics

select and cut
From the package of 10" print squares, select 26 squares. Cut each into 2½" strips and subcut each strip into 2½" squares. Each 10" square will yield (16) 2½" squares. A total of 416 squares are needed.

Note: if you've chosen to use yardage, cut (9) 2½" strips across the width of the fabric from each of 2 of the pieces you've chosen and (8) 2½" strips across the width of the fabric from the remaining piece. Subcut each strip into 2½" squares. Each strip will yield 16 squares and a total of 416 are needed.

layer and push
Layer (2) 2½" squares together with wrong sides facing. Pick up the chopstick and place the center of the squares over the small end. While hanging on to the fabric, use the chopstick to push the fabric firmly into the styrofoam wreath form. Continue adding fabric squares until the front of the wreath form is covered and as full as you like.

embellishments
For the Christmas wreath, consider adding miniature ornaments or bows. Decorate your Valentine wreath with a bow, hearts, or flowers. Stars are a welcome addition when it comes to decorating an Independence Day wreath. Let your imagination run wild!

Hang on your door and enjoy!

bargello

QUILT SIZE
50" X 61½"

QUILT TOP
1 roll of 2½" strips
  – the roll you choose must have
  at least 3 strips each of 12
  different color values.

Note: while you may have 3 pieces of red that
all appear to be the same color value, the
print may vary. That will work just fine!

¾ yards contrasting fabric

BORDER
¾ yard

BINDING
¾ yard or use left over 2½" strips to
make multi-colored binding

BACKING
3¼ yards – horizontal seam(s)

SAMPLE QUILT
Vintage Holiday by Bonnie and
Camille for Moda Fabrics

QUILTING PATTERN
Christmas Paisley

ONLINE TUTORIALS
msqc.co/holidayblock18

PATTERN
pg. 24

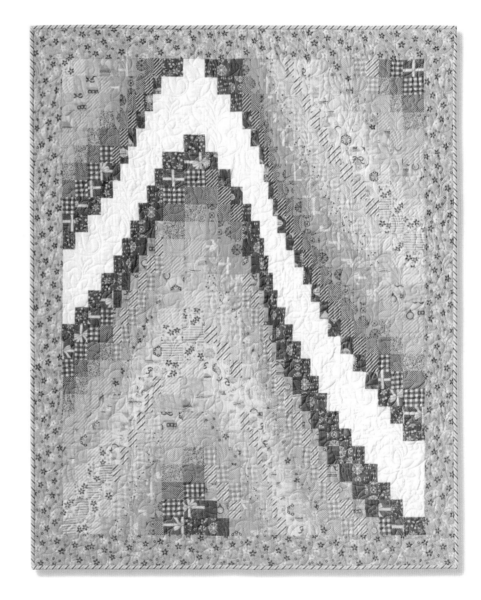

easy
half-hexagon

QUILT SIZE
55⅜" x 72¾"

BLOCK SIZE
4⅛" X 9½" finished

QUILT TOP
1 package 10" print squares

INNER BORDER
½ yard

OUTER BORDER
1¼ yards

BINDING
¾ yard

BACKING
3½ yards – horizontal seam(s)

OTHER
Missouri Star Quilt Co.
10" Half-Hexagon Template

SAMPLE QUILT
Let It Sparkle by RJR Studios
for RJR Fabrics

QUILTING PATTERN
Christmas Paisley

ONLINE TUTORIALS
msqc.co/holidayblock18

PATTERN
pg. 40

fall
shenanigans

QUILT SIZE
40½" x 40"

SUPPLIES
1 package 10" print squares
  - we used Halloween-themed fabric

½ yard background

BORDER
½ yard

BINDING
½ yard

BACKING
2½ yards - vertical seam(s)

OTHER
(1) 4½" x 6½" scrap of fusible
  – we used lightweight Heat 'n
Bond

Missouri Star Quilt Co. Large Simple
Wedge Template

SAMPLE QUILT
Spook-tacular Hues by Wilmington
Prints

QUILTING PATTERN
Spiderwebs

ONLINE TUTORIALS
msqc.co/holidayblock18

PATTERN
pg. 72

fence
rail stars

QUILT SIZE
43" X 43"

BLOCK SIZE
18" finished

SUPPLY LIST
1 roll of 2½" strips
1 yard background fabric – includes
  border

BINDING
½ yard

BACKING
3 yards - vertical seam(s)

SAMPLE QUILT
Pumpkin Patch Batik by Kathy Engle for
Island Batiks

QUILTING PATTERN
Pumpkins

ONLINE TUTORIALS
msqc.co/holidayblock18

PATTERN
pg. 66

grandmother's fan

QUILT SIZE
66" X 75½"

BLOCK SIZE
9½" finished

QUILT TOP
3 packages 5" print squares
1 package 42 ct. 10" background
  squares

BORDER
1½ yard – includes fabric for
  quarter circles at base of fans

BINDING
¾ yard

BACKING
4¾ yards – vertical seam(s)

ADDITIONAL SUPPLIES
Missouri Star Quilt Co. Large
  Dresden Plate Template

SAMPLE QUILT
Cats, Bats, and Jacks by My Mind's
Eye for Riley Blake Designs

QUILTING PATTERN
Spiderwebs

ONLINE TUTORIALS
msqc.co/holidayblock18

PATTERN
pg. 80

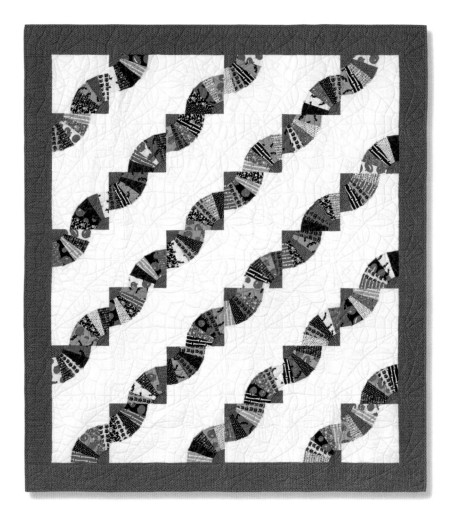

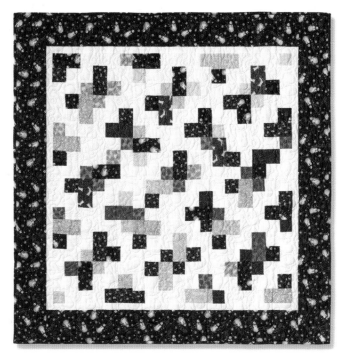

grand square
& do si do

QUILT SIZE
61″ x 61″

BLOCK SIZE
12″ finished

SUPPLIES
2 packages 5″ print squares -
    must include duplicate prints
2 yards background fabric -
    includes inner border

OUTER BORDER
1 yard

BINDING
¾ yard

BACKING
4 yards - vertical seam(s)

SAMPLE QUILT
Winter Wonderland by Cheryl Haynes
for Benartex Fabric

QUILTING PATTERN
Pine Tree Meander
Mitten Meander

ONLINE TUTORIALS
msqc.co/holidayblock18

PATTERN
pg. 6

josh's star

QUILT SIZE
73" x 73"

BLOCK SIZE
18" finished

SUPPLIES
1 package 10" print squares

SASHING AND INNER BORDER
1 yard

OUTER BORDER
1¼ yards

BINDING
¾ yard

BACKING
4½ yards - vertical seam(s)

OTHER
Missouri Star Quilt Co. Dresden
    Plate Template

SAMPLE QUILT
Holiday Flourish 11 by Peggy Toole
for Robert Kaufman

QUILTING PATTERN
Holly

ONLINE TUTORIALS
msqc.co/holidayblock18

PATTERN
pg. 48

rhombus star

QUILT SIZE
69½ x 90"

BLOCK SIZE
18½" X 20½" finished

QUILT TOP
1¾ yards white fabric
3¼ yards background fabric
  – includes inner border

OUTER BORDER
1½ yards

BINDING
¾ yard

BACKING
5½ yards – vertical seam(s)

OTHER
Missouri Star Quilt Co. 10" Rhombus
Template

SAMPLE QUILT
Kona Cotton White Yardage by
RK Studios for Robert Kaufman Lava
Sea Batik by Anthology Fabrics
and Essex Linen - Yarn Dyed
Oyster Metallic designed by Robert
Kaufman for Robert Kaufman Fabrics

NOTE: *The fabrics for this quilt may also be switched out for red and green to make a Christmas Rhombus Star.*

QUILTING PATTERN
Meander

ONLINE TUTORIALS
msqc.co/holidayblock18

PATTERN
pg. 56

town square

QUILT SIZE
68" X 86"

BLOCK SIZE
18" finished

QUILT TOP
1 roll 2½" print strips
1¾ yards black fabric – includes inner border

OUTER BORDER
1¼ yard

BINDING
¾ yard

BACKING
5¼ yards - vertical seam(s)

SAMPLE QUILT
Seeing Stars Grunge Metallics by BasicGrey for Moda Fabrics

QUILTING PATTERN
Stars and Loops

ONLINE TUTORIALS
msqc.co/holidayblock18

PATTERN
pg. 16

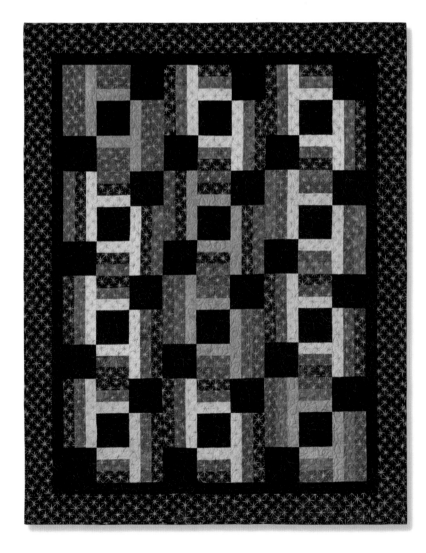

twinkling stars

QUILT SIZE
74" x 84"

BLOCK SIZE
8" finished

QUILT TOP
4 packages 5" print squares
3¼ yards solid green background fabric - includes sashing and inner border

OUTER BORDER
1½ yards

BINDING
¾ yard

BACKING
5¼ yards – vertical seam(s)

SAMPLE QUILT
Overnight Delivery by Sweetwater for Moda Fabrics

QUILTING PATTERN
Loops and Swirls

ONLINE TUTORIALS
msqc.co/holidayblock18

PATTERN
pg. 32

construction basics

general quilting

- All seams are ¼" inch unless directions specify differently.
- Cutting instructions are given at the point when cutting is required.
- Precuts are not prewashed; therefore do not prewash other fabrics in the project.
- All strips are cut width of fabric.
- Remove all selvages.

press seams

- Use a steam iron on the cotton setting.
- Press the seam just as it was sewn right sides together. This "sets" the seam.
- With dark fabric on top, lift the dark fabric and press back.
- The seam allowance is pressed toward the dark side. Some patterns may direct otherwise for certain situations.
- Follow pressing arrows in the diagrams when indicated.
- Press toward borders. Pieced borders may demand otherwise.
- Press diagonal seams open on binding to reduce bulk.

borders

- Always measure the quilt top 3 times before cutting borders.
- Start measuring about 4" in from each side and through the center vertically.
- Take the average of those 3 measurements.
- Cut 2 border strips to that size. Piece strips together if needed.
- Attach one to either side of the quilt.

- Position the border fabric on top as you sew. The feed dogs can act like rufflers. Having the border on top will prevent waviness and keep the quilt straight.
- Repeat this process for the top and bottom borders, measuring the width 3 times.
- Include the newly attached side borders in your measurements.
- Press toward the borders.

binding

find a video tutorial at: www.msqc.co/006

- Use 2½" strips for binding.
- Sew strips end-to-end into one long strip with diagonal seams, aka the plus sign method (next). Press seams open.
- Fold in half lengthwise wrong sides together and press.
- The entire length should equal the outside dimension of the quilt plus 15" - 20."

plus sign method

- Lay one strip across the other as if to make a plus sign right sides together.
- Sew from top inside to bottom outside corners crossing the intersections of fabric as you sew.
  Trim excess to ¼" seam allowance.
- Press seam open.

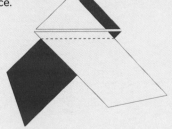

find a video tutorial at: www.msqc.co/001

attach binding

- Match raw edges of folded binding to the quilt top edge.
- Leave a 10" tail at the beginning.
- Use a ¼" seam allowance.
- Start in the middle of a long straight side.

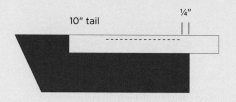

10" tail   ¼"

miter corners

- Stop sewing ¼" before the corner.
- Move the quilt out from under the presser foot.
- Clip the threads.
- Flip the binding up at a 90° angle to the edge just sewn.
- Fold the binding down along the next side to be sewn, aligning raw edges.
- The fold will lie along the edge just completed.
- Begin sewing on the fold.

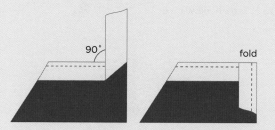

90°   fold

close binding

MSQC recommends The Binding Tool from TQM Products to finish binding perfectly every time.

- Stop sewing when you have 12" left to reach the start.
- Where the binding tails come together, trim excess leaving only 2½" of overlap.
- It helps to pin or clip the quilt together at the two points where the binding starts and stops. This takes the pressure off of the binding tails while you work.
- Use the plus sign method to sew the two binding ends together, except this time when making the plus sign, match the edges. Using a pencil, mark your sewing line because you won't be able to see where the corners intersect. Sew across.

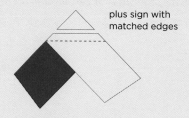

plus sign with matched edges

- Trim off excess; press seam open.
- Fold in half wrong sides together, and align all raw edges to the quilt top.
- Sew this last binding section to the quilt. Press.
- Turn the folded edge of the binding around to the back of the quilt and tack into place with an invisible stitch or machine stitch if you wish.